# LO

## The Why & How of Good Reproduction

*by*

G. A. BRIGGS

*Author of*

" SOUND REPRODUCTION "
" PIANOS, PIANISTS AND SONICS "

*and*

with H. H. GARNER

" AMPLIFIERS "
The Why and How of Good Amplification

ORIGINALLY
*Published by*

WHARFEDALE WIRELESS WORKS LTD.
IDLE . BRADFORD . YORKSHIRE . ENGLAND

AGENTS
AUDIO AMATEUR PRESS
Peterborough New Hampshire USA
Sales Agents: Old Colony Sound Lab
Post Office Box 243, Peterborough, NH 03458 USA

*First Edition*
*May 1948*

*Second Edition*
*December 1948*

*Third Edition*
*March 1949*

*Reprinted September 1949*
*,, November ,,*
*,, February 1950*
*,, June ,,*
*,, May 1951*
*,, February 1952*
*,, October ,,*
*,, May 1953*
*,, September ,,*

*Fourth Edition*
*January 1955*

*Reprinted October 1955*



Reprinted, with permission, Wharfedale, Ltd.,
Sandleas Way, Crossgates, Leeds LS15 8AL, United Kingdom

Second Reprint Edition
1990


ISBN: 0-9624191-3-3
Library of Congress Card Catalog Number: 90-081199

# CONTENTS

## ILLUSTRATIONS



## ACKNOWLEDGMENTS


Thanks are due to the authors and publishers named below for permission to reproduce the illustrations mentioned.

Figures 1, 17, 24, 26, 31 and 32 from Olson's "Elements of Acoustical Engineering". *D. Van Nostrand Co. Inc.*

Figures 5, 9, 18, 21, 23 and 28 from Henney's "Radio Engineering Handbook" *McGraw Hill Book Co. Inc.*

Figure 30 from Wood's "Physics of Music". *Methuen & Co. Ltd.*

Figures 10 and 11 from Seashore's "Psychology of Music". *McGraw Hill Book Co. Inc.*

Figure 9A from Olson & Massa's "Applied Acoustics". *The Blakiston Co.*

Figure 36 from Wood's "Sound Waves and their Uses". *Blackie & Son, Ltd*

Figure 27 by permission of R.C.A. Photophone Ltd.

# INTRODUCTION

Since the end of the war, there has been a marked increase in the interest shown in better quality of reproduction of radio and records.

This is probably due to three main causes—

1. During the war (and the black-out) many people turned their attention to good music and began to enjoy it for the first time.
2. Thousands of men in the forces had advanced radio experience.
3. Troops in Italy and other countries listened to operas and orchestras and many have returned home with a new interest in life—serious music.

On the lighter side, people who appreciate and enjoy a first-class dance band are beginning to listen for the true note of the double bass and the sizzling of the snare drums.

This little book is therefore intended for those who, for reasons similar to those mentioned above, are interested in the Loudspeaker and how it works, and how results may be improved. The present scarcity and high cost of timber and plywood also account for a good deal of interest in home construction.

My qualifications for writing this booklet are not very extensive, as I am neither a scientist nor a mathematician, but I have been making loudspeakers for fifteen years, and all my life I have been fascinated by sound. In my search for the perfect piano, more than three dozen uprights and grands have darkened my door during the last 30 years. My hobby is music and I make a practice of attending concerts and playing the piano regularly in order to keep my hearing fresh, as I think that the tonal quality of music is quite as important as its melodic and harmonic structure. My approach to the subject is, therefore, as much from the musical angle as from the technical.

The book is written in non-technical terms throughout, and many readers may find some chapters extremely elementary. Nevertheless I hope they will be patient for the sake of those who have no knowledge or experience of the subjects concerned, for whom the book is primarily intended.

I am indebted to the following people for kind and generous help—

Mr. F. Keir Dawson for drawing and preparing many blocks

Mr. F. Beaumont, chief engineer of Ambassador Radio, for reading proofs and correcting and supplying technical details.

My wife for patiently reading manuscript and eliminating a good deal of padding.

Members of my staff who have cheerfully made weird and wonderful models for purposes of test.

My thanks are also due to the Publishers who have so readily consented to the use of Diagrams and Tables from other books, to which I have liberally and unblushingly helped myself. I should like to place on record the friendly and generous attitude of the three American Publishers listed, which is a small but significant example of the goodwill which exists in the U.S.A. towards this country. The following books are strongly recommended to those who wish to go further into the subjects—

1. The Physics of Music, by A Wood (Methuen).
2. Psychology of Music, by Seashore (McGraw-Hill).
3. Elements of Acoustical Engineering, Olson (Chapman and Hall).
4. Radio Engineering Handbook, Henney (McGraw-Hill).

I am most anxious that anything I say in this booklet should not be taken as a reflection on set makers, as I fully appreciate that they are compelled by circumstances to provide selectivity, convenient size and attractive appearance, in addition to lively performance, and these attributes are not always compatible with best local station quality.

G. A. Briggs

# FOREWORD to FOURTH EDITION

The response to this "pithy pamphlet", as one American reviewer described it, has been so good that the First Edition was sold out in less than five months and the second edition went in about two months. The Third Edition was reprinted eight times, bringing the total sales to 41,000 copies to date. Nearly half of these have gone to the U.S.A. and Canada. 7,000 copies of the Fourth Edition have now been printed, making a total publication figure of 48,000 to date.

As the book deals mainly with the fundamentals of loudspeaker design and use, the necessity for constant revision does not arise.

In this, the Fourth Edition, there has been no serious alteration to the text, apart from a reference to sound reproduction in the Royal Festival Hall on page 60, the power in watts used in the hall and in the home with details of a simple watt indicating device on page 79, and the insertion of details of a three-way crossover unit on page 65. The Supplement has been brought up to date by the inclusion of a description of the Electrostatic Speaker and the French Elipson design.

The original Introduction is still retained, as it explains why the book was written in the first place; but my 15 years of speaker-making must now be extended to 22 years. *Tempus fugit.*

A reference to the later book, "SOUND REPRODUCTION", would not be out of place here, as it should be of interest to readers who wish to extend their investigations in the high fidelity field. First published in 1949, the book is now in the second impression of its Third Edition, with a total publication figure just short of 40,000. This book tries hard to overtake the reprints of "LOUDSPEAKERS", but at double the price it is uphill work. As it contains four times as many pages it is actually cheaper from a paper and print point of view.

January 1955 G. A. B.

A French Edition of "Sound Reproduction" has been published by Société des Editions Radio, Paris, under the title of "Reproduction Sonore à Haute Fidélité."

"Loudspeakers" has been translated into French and Dutch and is published by P. H. Brans Ltd., Antwerp, Belgium.

The book "Amplifiers" is now out of print.

*How sour sweet music is,*

*When time is broke and no proportion kept !*

*So is it with the music of men's lives.*

KING RICHARD II

## CHAPTER I

# QUALITY of REPRODUCTION and DISTORTION

During the recent B.B.C. Jubilee programmes, when listeners were taken behind the scenes at Broadcasting House, it was frankly admitted that everything in Radio is a compromise. It will help in the study of loudspeakers if the reader will bear in mind that compromise enters into every aspect of the problem. There is no perfect loudspeaker, but we will assume that the objective is to get as near to the original as possible. We will ignore impracticable suggestions such as binaural transmission and reception, listening in sound-proof "dead" rooms with no ventilation, or sitting in the mouth of a huge exponential horn some fifteen or twenty feet square.

There is, however, another side to the question of quality which is so ably described by SEASHORE in "PSYCHOLOGY OF MUSIC" that we cannot do better than quote as follows —

> "The engineering development in the control of the dynamics of tone in recording, reproducing and broadcasting is one of the most important contributions that has ever been made to the popularizing of music.
>
> "In recording, for example, not only can the man at the instrument change instantly the loudness of the tone as a whole, but he can deal with any particular element of the tone selectively in such a way as to improve upon the performance of the instrument or the voice. This is called building up the tone."

No doubt many readers can recall instances where they have been disappointed on hearing a singer in person after hearing the same artist by radio or records. Nevertheless, in spite of this building up of tone, we still have to strive for natural results in reproduction, and it is possible to obtain better tonal quality but with an absence of naturalness, which seems to depend on the very high frequencies.

It is claimed by some experts that for really life-like results, frequencies up to 30,000 are necessary, because, although the average human ear cuts off at about 16,000 cycles, the difference-tones are heard. This means that if two tones of 20,000 and 30,000 cycles are produced, the difference-tone of 10,000 cycles may be heard, and its absence takes something away from the quality. All this is probably true, but these high frequencies are not available today.

It is probable that Frequency Modulation will produce a wider range than the present limit of 10,000 cycles in broadcasting, and improvements will no doubt be made in recording so that high frequencies are not completely swamped by surface noise. The power used at H.F. levels is very small, and a high tone is quickly massed by a low one. This explains why needle scratch is inaudible during low note passages of music, and increasing the low frequency output of a speaker appears to cut the top.

For the purposes of this book we will try to deal with the situation as it is and not as it ought to be. Let us look on the Loudspeaker as a musical instrument as well as a piece of wireless equipment, and if the very high frequencies have greater annoyance value than musical merit, discard them.

The average commercial receiver still cuts off at about 5,000 cycles.

## DISTORTION

There are numerous causes of distortion in loud speakers, which are referred to in the chapters on Cones, Centring devices, Volume and Watts, Cabinets, Transients, Crossover networks, Feedback, Transformers and Phase effects.

Two special forms of distortion are dealt with in the following paragraphs—

The Transient or Delayed Action characteristic is a source of distortion which has been investigated by the Research Department of the B.B.C., and may be described as the unequal duration of vibrations at different frequencies. Tests are made by interrupting the A.F. signal at regular intervals of time and taking a sort of delayed-action response curve. Presumably, the non-uniform rate of decay at different frequencies is due to resonances in the vibrating system, which intensify the reverberation period.

There is one aspect of harmonic distortion which should be borne in mind. It is found that high frequency harmonic distortion is much more noticeable than harmonic distortion at medium and low freqnencies. According to Olson, in "Elements of Acoustical Engineering," 5% second harmonic and 3% third harmonic are noticeable on equipment with uniform response from 45 to 8,500 cycles, but in the case of the higher harmonics introduced by Class B or pentode output a fraction of one per cent. is noticeable. It follows, therefore, that a loudspeaker with extended H.F. response will expose harmonic distortion in the frequency range where it is most objectionable to the ear, and such speakers should only be used on equipment which is above suspicion.

## CHAPTER I

# DEVELOPMENT OF LOUDSPEAKERS

Although the moving-coil or electro-dynamic type is now almost exclusively used, it is no doubt worth while to look at the five main electro-acoustic driving systems which have been used.

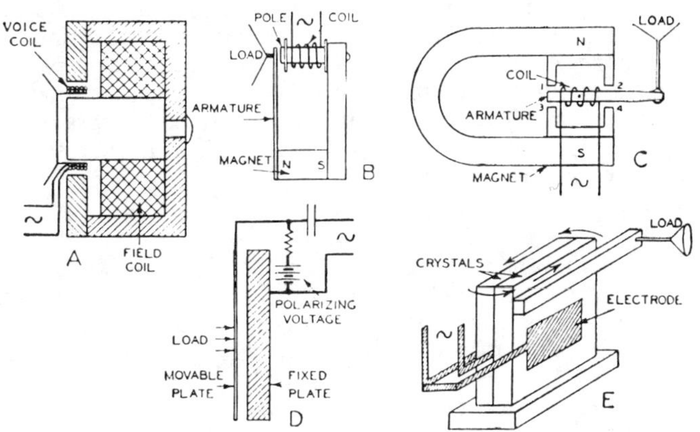


FIG. 1—DRIVING SYSTEMS.
A electro dynamic—moving coil.
B electro magnetic—moving iron.
C electro-magnetic—balanced armature.
D condenser.
E crystal.

*From Olson, Elements of Acoustical Engineering*

**A.**—The response range and comparatively level impedance of the moving-coil system, coupled with low production costs, have established its superiority over all its rivals. (*See Fig.* 6, *Page* 21.)

**B.**—Moving-iron type. This consists of a permanent magnet operating directly upon a ferrous armature. Most of the earliest loudspeakers were based on this system. Reproduction was marred by reed resonance, distortion and absence of bass.

**C.**—Balanced armature. A definite improvement on the previous type, the balanced armature was extensively used about 18/20 years ago. It was not found possible to reduce the stiffness of the armature sufficiently to give bass response below 120 cycles.

**D.**—Condenser. This type has been used as a loudspeaker, with the plate radiating directly into the air. Its poor impedance characteristic and the necessity for high polarizing voltage proved serious drawbacks and its popularity was short-lived.

E.—Piezoelectric Driving System. The bending and twisting properties of certain crystals with applied E.M.F's are well known, and are in regular use in microphones and pick-ups. The system has been applied to loudspeakers for high note reproduction, where the impedance characteristic appears to be favourable and awakening interest in extreme H.F. response may direct attention once more in this direction. The crystal is not easily adapted for bass reproduction on account of the large movements which are necessary in a loudspeaker at low frequencies.

## MOVING COIL SYSTEM

It is clear that the moving-coil system has no serious rival. Early types were fitted with high resistance voice coils, leather suspension and mains-energised magnets, mostly replaced today by low resistance coils with matching transformer, corrugated cones and permanent magnets. High resistance coils were wound with the finest enamelled wire, (46 or even 47 S.W.G.) for use in the plate circuit of the output valve. The casualty rate was very high, both during production and use, and no tears were shed at the total demise of this type, some 12/14 years ago. Today, voice coils of 2/3 ohms for domestic use and 15 ohms for public address are almost universally used.

The change from leather or other flexible surround to moulded corrugations was a very important factor in reducing the cost of production and certainly brought about large-scale adoption of the moving-coil unit, thus striking the death knell of previous electro-magnetic systems. The effect on quality of reproduction was more questionable, as it is now realised that the apparent increase in efficiency (volume) was due to increased resonance, and much of the true bass was lost by stiffness in the suspension. Improvements have, however, been made in both these directions, and great skill is now used in producing cones having predetermined resonance points.

As regards the third change from mains-energised to permanent magnets, no one can doubt the efficiency of the modern P.M., and its convenience in use is self-evident.

The two extreme ends of the audio-frequency band are always the most difficult to transmit, to record and to reproduce with the same efficiency as the middle register. It is fairly easy to make a moving-coil loudspeaker to cover 80 to 8,000 cycles without serious loss, but to extend the range to 30 cycles in the bass and 15,000 in the extreme top presents quite a few problems. Inefficiency in the bass is due mainly to low radiation resistance, while the mass of the vibrating system reduces efficiency in the extreme top. A large cone increases the radiation resistance and improves bass response, but the resulting increase in weight leads to poorer H.F. response. Various ways of meeting and overcoming these difficulties are dealt with in other chapters, but for domestic use the most successful combination of bass and treble in a single unit appears to be attained in a speaker of about 10 inches diameter.

## CHAPTER III

# MAGNETS

In the early models of moving-coil speakers the magnetic force was obtained by electric current in a large field coil, as much as 40 watts being dissipated in the biggest units. These electro-dynamic speakers are often referred to briefly as mains-energised, or merely energised. It was impossible in those days to attain by permanent magnets the high flux densities developed in large energised magnets, and even medium efficiency required large and costly permanent magnets.

## PERMANENT MAGNETS

These have been improved so enormously during the last 15 years that they are today always used, unless the conditions are such that it is more economical to use a field coil—for the double purpose of energising and smoothing.

We can, therefore, confine our remarks to permanent magnets. Research has been concentrated on reduction in weight, size and cost, with longer life, or in one word—efficiency. How successful this has been will be seen from the following drawings, illustrating the size and weight of magnet required for a flux density of 7,000 lines in a gap .040″ wide on a centre pole 1″ in diameter.

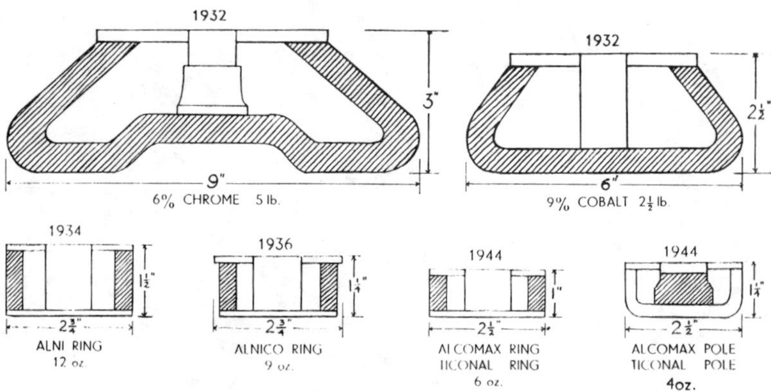


FIG. 2—APPROXIMATE SIZE AND WEIGHT OF MAGNET FOR EQUAL PERFORMANCE
ALNI=Aluminium and Nickel.
ALNICO=Aluminium, Nickel and Cobalt.
ALCOMAX=Treated in Magnetic Field.
British Alcomax III is equivalent to American Alnico 5.

The life of a modern magnet is so long that the title Permanent is hardly a misnomer, and the magnet can at any time be re-magnetised equal to new.

## FLUX DENSITY

It is possible to attain maximum flux densities without much difficulty, and limitations are now set by saturation of the mild steel parts. With a one inch centre pole, saturation occurs at 14,000 lines, and it is not economically possible to exceed this figure without reducing the size of the gap. With a ¾″ centre pole and normal gap dimensions, saturation starts at 9,000 lines.[1]

It is not possible to assess the value of a magnet merely by reference to the flux density per sq. centimetre. Attention should also be paid to the total flux, as it is obviously feasible to increase the flux density per sq. centimetre by using thinner steel plates or reducing the gap area. Such a change might not be an improvement ; it would depend on the design and purpose of the speaker.

Using the same thickness of plate, a magnet giving 8,000 lines on a 1″ centre pole would be superior to a magnet giving 9,000 lines on a ¾″ pole.

The centre block type of magnet is being developed, especially for television sets, as it has no external field. It is the most economical design yet devised so far as weight of magnet is concerned, for small and medium types.

The cost of magnets increases rapidly when higher flux densities are involved. The flux density does not go up in proportion to the increase in weight, and after a certain performance is attained, each increment of 1,000 lines becomes more and more difficult to achieve. This accounts for the comparatively high prices charged for loudspeakers with high flux density. The approximate weight of magnet casting required for various flux readings on one inch pole are given for comparison—

8,000 lines, 8 ozs of Alcomax,
10,000 ,, 12 ozs. ,, ,,
12,000 ,, 20 ozs. ,, ,,
14,000 ,, 56 ozs. ,, ,,

Apart from improving sensitivity, high flux density increases the damping on the voice coil and gives life and attack to the reproduction with wider response range, and improved power handling capacity at low frequencies.

(1) Saturation of the pole is the main obstacle to high efficiency in small speakers with ½″ or ¾″ voice-coil. A larger unit with 1″ centre pole is easily designed to give much higher flux density and obviously greater total flux, with far superior performance at high frequencies.

## CHAPTER IV

# CHASSIS OR CONE HOUSING

In order to maintain the position of the cone, to hold the speech coil centrally in the magnet gap, and also to anchor the centring spider, it is necessary to have some sort of rigid frame-work.

As the clearance between the coil and magnet is usually not more than .010″ and may be as low as .005″, it will be realised that any bending or "give" in the chassis, however slight, may throw the coil out of centre and cause a rattle.

Chassis are generally made in pressed steel or die-cast aluminium alloys. The pressed steel variety is almost invariably used for mass production on account of low cost, and is quite reliable so long as the quality and gauge of metal are adequate. It is, however, worth noting that with the average steel chassis it is possible to distort the shape by using too much pressure when bolting to baffle or cabinet, and to throw the speech coil out of alignment. Fixing nuts should therefore only be reasonably tight.

Die-cast chassis are more costly than pressed steel, and are liable to fracture, but have the advantages of greater rigidity, less resonance, accurate dimensions, and open construction.

When a loudspeaker is mounted in a small cabinet, or in a wireless set surrounded by valves and components, the partial enclosure of the cone by the usual pressed steel chassis is of little or no consequence, but where acoustic loading on the back of the cone is involved, an open design of chassis is necessary.

The effect of chassis resonance was pointed out by the *Wireless World* in a series of loudspeaker tests made as far back as 1935.

CHAPTER V.

# CONES

The design and construction of the cone play a most important part in the performance of a loudspeaker, affecting volume, range, clarity and power-handling capacity. The majority are now made in seamless moulded paper from special dies to very accurate dimensions.

The performance of a cone is affected by its size, shape, weight, texture and corrugations. Generally speaking, the cone which produces the greatest volume gives the worst quality. As the objective is lightness with rigidity, the straight-sided cone is generally adopted, but curved or exponential cones are sometimes used. This shape improves high note response, but in some cases reduces power-handling capacity.

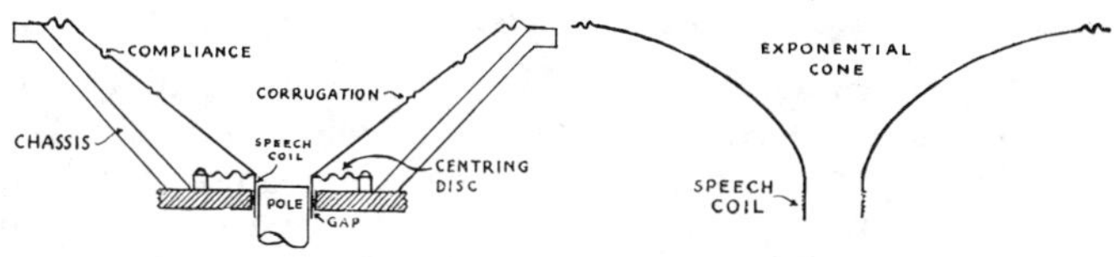


FIG. 3

SECTIONAL VIEW OF CONE ASSEMBLY. CURVED CONE.

Elliptical cones are sometimes used, both with straight and curved sides, and have certain acoustic properties which differ from the usual circular shape, but low-note efficiency is inferior. An elliptical speaker should be mounted with its major axis vertical in order to get the widest horizontal distribution of high notes, in the same way that a small speaker radiates over a wider angle than a big one at H.F.

## CORRUGATIONS

The corrugations around the periphery control the fundamental resonance, and the frequency can be lowered by making the corrugations thinner—a point of considerable importance.

A common fault in loudspeaker cones is the development of sub-harmonics. When a pure tone in the upper register is introduced with sufficient power, an extra note is produced by the cone at a lower frequency. Some people hold that this is of no consequence, as this steady tone condition is never arrived at in normal use.

This may be true, but the fact remains that a cone which breaks up badly into sub-harmonics belongs to the "loud" variety, and gives poor definition in orchestral effects. In any case there is little need today to select a cone or speaker for domestic use on account of its loudness, as most wireless sets provide ample volume.

Mid-cone corrugations are often employed. A corrugation may be inserted to add rigidity to the cone in a radial direction and subdue the sub-harmonics mentioned above. Other corrugations may act as compliances to subdue or arrest the top note vibrations.

## CONE ACTION

A cone moves as a piston at frequencies below the lowest mode of the cone itself, unless the surround or suspension is so stiff as to cause the cone to flex even at low frequencies. Such flexing distorts the low notes and increases loudness at harmonic frequencies, and intermodulation between treble and bass occurs, with inevitable rough and unpleasant top note response.

The frequency at which a cone ceases to act as a piston is about 1,000 cycles in an 8″ cone, and at this frequency all parts of the cone move in phase. The displacement is greatest at the apex and least at the periphery, where the transmission line terminates. The impedance of this termination is very important.

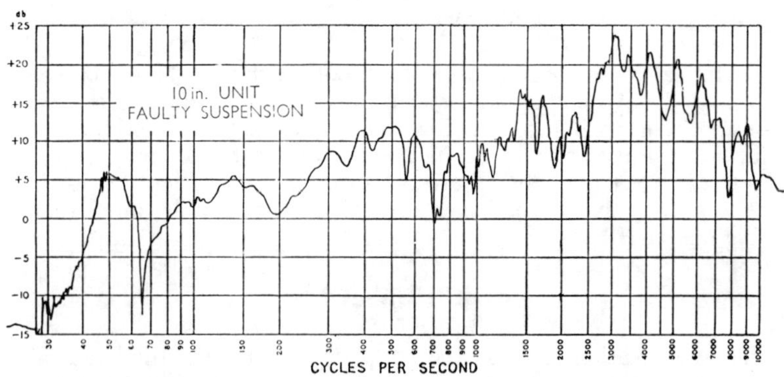


Fig. 4—Response Curve of 10″ Speaker with uneven suspension affecting bass, and bakelized apex affecting H.F. output.

Fig. 4 shows the drop in bass response resulting from uneven pressure around the periphery of a cone caused by upward pressure from the centring device. The dip in the bass was removed by levelling the surround and elevation.

At frequencies higher than the above mode, the cone vibrates in sections, and the region of the apex plays a more and more important part as the frequency rises. The apex is often specially treated, and Fig 4 also shows the effect of actually bakelizing this portion of a ten-inch paper cone.

## DIAMETER

The size of a cone is also a question of some importance. The low note efficiency increases with size at the rate of about an octave per four inches diameter for the same movement, Fig. 5. It is also much easier to keep the fundamental resonance at a low frequency with a bigger and heavier cone, but the extreme top becomes more difficult.

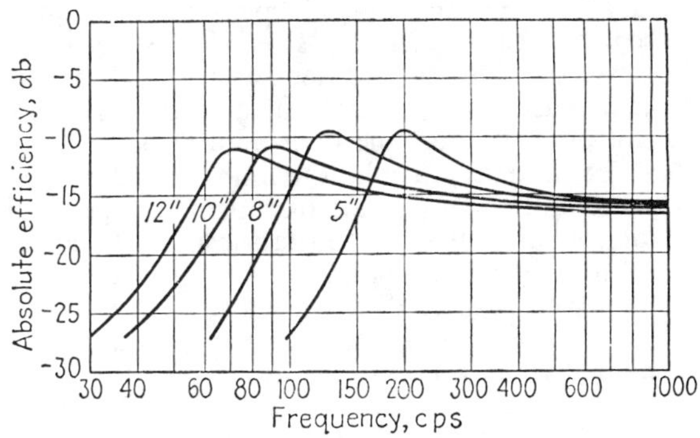


FIG. 5—Efficiency of Four Speakers of different size with same magnet.

*From Henneys Radio Engineering Handbook*

All cones are directional at high frequencies, but in this respect a small cone is better than a large one, as its high note radiation covers a wider angle. The small cone is also more efficient at high frequencies, with the same flux density, but it should be remembered that small speakers are usually fitted with small magnets resulting in lower acoustic output.

## FREQUENCY DOUBLING

This is the most common fault in a loudspeaker, and usually occurs at all frequencies below the main cone resonance, although it can be caused at higher frequencies by incorrect loading, such as an unsuitable horn. Where the fault occurs, the speaker produces a note an octave or more higher than the input, which often sounds more like a rattle than a musical tone. True bass reproduction in the region of frequency doubling is quite impossible.

## CHAPTER VI

# CENTRING DEVICES

In view of the small gap in which a speech coil is expected to vibrate without fouling the magnet, some form of centring device is essential.

A perfect device would prevent all lateral movement of the coil, would help to retain its correct elevation when at rest in the gap, but would not impose increasing restraint as the piston movement of the coil develops, and would not have any self-resonance.

The first two of these qualities are fairly practicable, but the second two are not so easy, and we must still look on the centring device as a necessary evil.

In the early days of moving-coil speakers front spiders were generally used, but have been almost entirely superseded by rear suspension devices. The back spider—as it is called—is superior for three main reasons—(a) it is located nearer the actual coil ; (b) it does not directly affect the high note response of the cone ; and (c) it can be designed with longer limbs to reduce restraint at maximum deflection. Many kinds of tough paper and fibre have been used for spiders, but bakelised fabric is now widely used on account of its non-hygroscopic and resilient qualities.

Moulded paper corrugated discs have also been extensively used, and are attractive for closing the magnetic gap against dust and filings. Similar discs in a fabric material are now being produced and have distinct advantages, such as greater flexibility and resilience with less resonance.[1] The equal radial pressure of the corrugations is also a safeguard against non-linearity at cone resonance.

Distortion will be caused at low frequencies by the centring device if it is mounted in such a way that unequal radial or piston pressure is exerted on the cone and coil assembly, or if the the amplitude of piston movement is excessive. Such distortion is mostly third harmonic.

---

(1) **Centring Devices.** The type of device used has a marked effect on the L.F. output of the speaker. Corrugated discs tend to reduce the resonance peak and widen its frequency range. In some cases the bass is increased by a sort of drum effect, giving woolly reproduction. The bakelised spider gives a sharply defined bass resonance to the cone, resulting in a crispness in the tone which is favoured by many designers.

## CHAPTER VII

# IMPEDANCE

The speech coil of a moving-coil speaker has inductance as well as resistance, which means, in plain language, that its resistance to alternating current varies according to the frequency of the current, and therefore, for a given applied E.M.F., the current flowing in the coil will vary with frequency. This form of A.C. resistance is known as Impedance. The impedance characteristic of the M. C. speaker is far superior to other types of reproducer, as a glance at Fig. 6 will show.

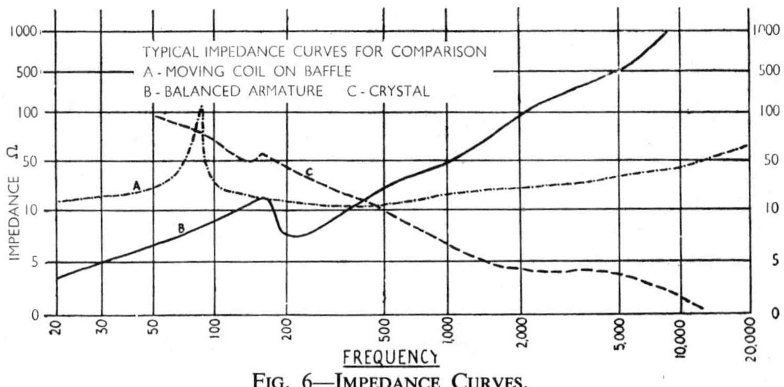


FIG. 6—IMPEDANCE CURVES.

The impedance of a loudspeaker is usually measured by comparing the voltage developed across the speech coil at different frequencies with the voltage across a known resistance, by means of a valve voltmeter.

Broadly speaking, the impedance curve can be taken as a measure of the superiority of the moving-coil speaker over all its rivals, and its importance in considering the performance of any model cannot be over-emphasised.

The impedance of the speaker is also affected by mechanical considerations, such as the cone resonance, the air loading imposed by the method of mounting, and vibrations of cabinet.

Whereas response curves vary enormously according to the method of taking them, and may even require a pinch of salt to aid digestion, an impedance curve at a given volume level can be accepted as a statement of fact. It may also be said that any alteration to design, or the method of mounting, which improves the impedance curve of a loudspeaker generally improves its performance (artificial loading excluded).

It is, of course, necessary to know the impedance of a speaker in order to match the load, but this is dealt with under the heading of Transformers. As the impedance varies with frequency, it is impossible to have so-called accurate matching, and it is usual to accept the impedance at a frequency between 400 and 1,000 cycles as a representative value. Where the speaker impedance is not known, it may be taken as 30/50% higher than the D.C. resistance of the voice coil.

The two main defects of the moving-coil speaker are the rising impedance in the treble and the hump in the bass at the fundamental resonance. These are clearly shown in Fig 7/A. The first of these is countered by various cone arrangements and modifications, or by employing two cones, two coils, or two speakers. The effect of using two speakers with a crossover at about 1,000 cycles is shown in Fig. 34, page 65, where the curve remains fairly level between 1,000 and 5,000 cycles instead of rising sharply.

Now whereas the rising impedance in the treble leads to loss of output unless counteracted, the rise in the bass signifies increased acoustic output as it arises from mechanical resonance, and one way to deal with it is to make a virtue of necessity and use it for reinforcing bass response, provided it occurs at a sufficiently low frequency. The resonance can quite easily be eliminated by electrical or mechanical damping, but audible results do not seem to justify such drastic treatment. It is often an advantage to cut out part of the bass resonance by negative feed-back, and make use of the remainder. The effect of Reflex loading is shown in Fig. 7, where the hump in the bass is reduced by 50%, the fundamental resonance is lowered by 20 cycles, and the wave form between 30 and 75 is audibly improved.

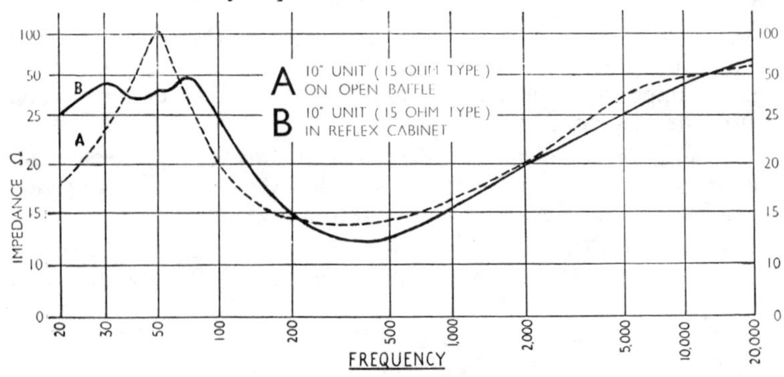


Fig. 7—Impedance Curves to Show improvements due to Reflex Loading Cabinet used 30″ × 15″ × 12″.

It will be appreciated that the cone movement at low frequencies in curve 7/B is much less than in curve A, and there is no pronounced peak. This reduces distortion, eliminates one note bass effects, and increases power-handling capacity.

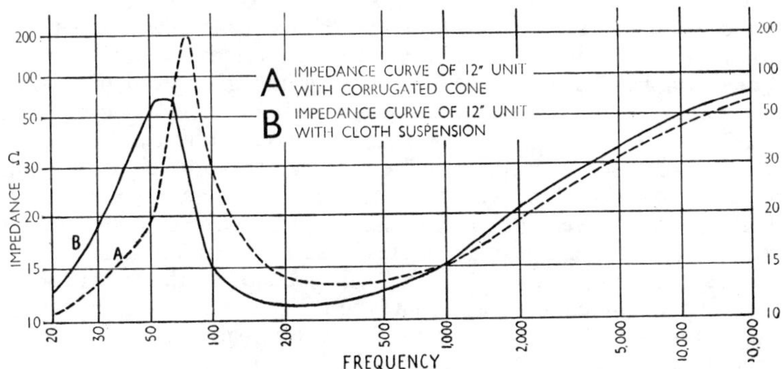


FIG. 8—Impedance Curves to show effect of soft suspension.

An impedance test also shows the effect on bass resonance resulting from fitting a soft surround to a cone in place of the usual corrugations, see Fig. 8. Here again the peak voltage is reduced and the hump in the curve has a wider base and occurs at a lower frequency. (See Transient Response, Chapter xvii.).

CHAPTER VIII

# PHONS AND DECIBELS

The Phon is a unit of measurement of loudness which allows for the difference in sensitivity of the ear at different frequencies. One phon is about the smallest increase of loudness which can be noticed under ordinary conditions. Every time the intensity of sound waves is doubled, the loudness increases by about 3 phons. For example, if a wireless set is working and giving out 60 phons, and another set is turned on at the same volume level, the combined loudness will be 63 phons. Similarly, if you connect an extension speaker to a set you approximately halve the volume in the main speaker, or in other words reduce the loudness by 3 phons. Unfortunately, even the phon does not agree with the ear's idea of loudness, and there is no recognised scale based on this. When you reduce volume level by half, the impression in the ear is that it has only been reduced by about one-fifth, and this peculiarity of hearing has certainly helped in the widespread use of extension speakers.

According to Alexander Wood, in "The Physics of Music", the range of power from a full orchestra playing *ff* to the solo violin playing *pp* is in the ratio of about twenty million to one.

This does not mean twenty million times as loud, because the intensity of the sensation of hearing is proportional not to the stimulus but to the logarithm of the stimulus. Thus equal increments of loudness are obtained, not by adding, but by multiplying by the same factor—so that 10 to 100, 100 to 1,000, and 1,000 to 10,000 are equal increments. The same law applies to frequencies, where each octave is double the one below.

Hence the necessity for a logarithmic basis for the decibel and the phon.

In the book mentioned above, Mr. Wood also says : There seems little reason to doubt that in future the phon scale for loudness will replace the indefinite *p* and *f* marking on the music score. Already Stokowski uses a phon meter, and interprets his score as

| | | | |
|---|---|---|---|
| *ppp* | 20 phons | *f* | 75 phons |
| *pp* | 40 ,, | *ff* | 85 ,, |
| *p* | 55 ,, | *fff* | 95 ,, |
| *mf* | 65 ,, | | |

One can see the usefulness of this marking for recording and broadcasting purposes, as the conductor could be responsible for controlling maximum and minimum volume levels without interference by an engineer, and no doubt this would give a more artistic result to the listener.

A further list from "Physics of Music" gives the power actually radiated as sound by various musical instruments—

| *Source* | *Loudness* | *Power in Watts* |
|---|---|---|
| Orchestra of 75 | .. maximum | 70 |
| Bass Drum .. | .. ,, | 25 |
| Pipe Organ .. | .. ,, | 13 |
| Snare Drum .. | .. ,, | 12 |
| Cymbals .. | .. ,, | 10 |
| Trombone .. | .. ,, | 6 |
| Piano .. .. | .. ,, | 0.4 |
| Saxophone .. | .. ,, | 0.3 |
| Bass Tuba .. | .. ,, | 0.2 |
| Double Bass .. | .. ,, | 0.16 |
| Piccolo .. | .. ,, | 0.08 |
| Flute .. .. | .. ,, | 0.06 |
| Clarinet .. | .. ,, | 0.05 |
| French Horn .. | .. ,, | 0.05 |
| Triangle .. | .. ,, | 0.05 |
| Bass Voice .. | .. ,, | 0.03 |
| Alto Voice .. | .. *p p* | 0.001 |
| Speech.. .. | .. Average | 0.000024 |
| Violin .. .. | .. Softest | 0.0000038 |

The difficulty of recording and broadcasting both extremes of loudness will be appreciated. The following readings with a Phon-meter are included for purposes of comparison—

| | *Meter Reading* |
|---|---|
| Orchestral record, about 10 Watts to speaker .. | 98 db. |
| Soprano record, full domestic volume .. .. | 80 ,, |
| Needle scratch, same output as above .. .. | 47 ,, |
| ,, ,, ,, ,, centre groove .. | 54 ,, |
| ,, ,, ,, ,, acetate disc .. | 40 ,, |
| Piano, 7′ 6″ grand, full volume .. .. .. | 90 ,, |
| ,, ,, ,, bottom C loud .. .. | 87 ,, |
| ,, ,, ,, middle C ,, .. .. | 83 ,, |
| ,, ,, ,, top C ,, .. .. | 67 ,, |
| Typewriting machine .. .. .. .. | 60 ,, |
| Normal speech .. .. .. .. .. | 60 ,, |
| Quiet speech.. .. .. .. .. .. | 50 ,, |
| Inside car, motor idling .. .. .. .. | 58 ,, |
| ,, ,, travelling uphill at 30 m.p.h. .. | 78 ,, |
| Very quiet room .. .. .. .. . | 30 ,, |

The needle scratch could be heard with the soprano, but not with the orchestra. The acetate scratch level of 40 db. is inaudible on all but the quietest passages. The motor car noise of 78 db. is too high for comfortable listening, but 58 db. is about equal to needle scratch.

A very loud sound seems almost equally loud from 30 to 6,000 cycles, as shown in Fig 9, but as the intensity is reduced the loudness falls off rapidly below 400 cycles and soon becomes inaudible below 60 cycles.

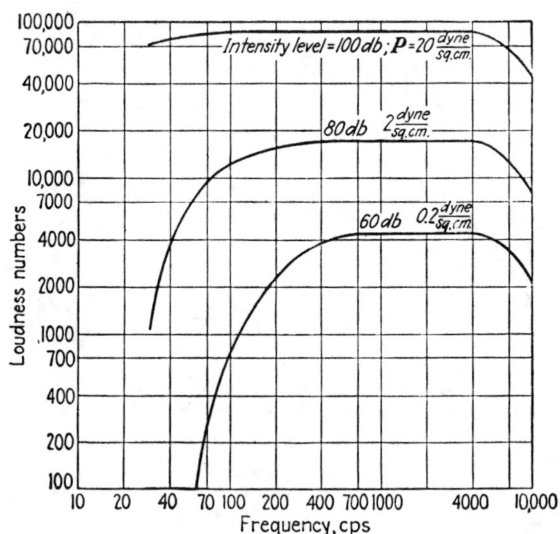


FIG. 9—Loudness Variation with frequency for three pure tones of the indicated intensity.

*From Henney's Radio Engineering Handbook*

The ear is most sensitive to frequencies between 2,000 and 5,000 cycles, and gradually less sensitive towards extreme bass and extreme top. It follows, therefore, that the same frequency response in amplifiers and loudspeakers will not suit all volume levels.

Considerable improvement to low-level reproduction of music can be achieved by using a three-channel amplifier where the extreme bass and top can be increased independently of the middle register.

Alternatively, a "straight" set or amplifier with a tone control to suppress the middle would answer the same purpose.

On the other hand, the reproduction of speech is often enhanced by reducing bass response, and where articulation is more important than naturalness the response range can be limited to 600/4,000 cycles.

## DECIBELS

In acoustics the ranges of intensities are so large that it is convenient to use a scale of smaller numbers termed decibels (abbreviation db.), based upon a logarithmic basis.

The decibel is not a measure for defining any voltage or power ; it is an expression for comparing them. It is generally used for response curves, as it gives a comparison of the outputs at different frequencies regardless of the actual power level at which the tests are made.

The only difference between the decibel and the phon is that the latter is regulated to correspond to the sensitivity of hearing at different frequencies.

| *Frequency* | *D.B. above threshold* | | *Phons* | *D.B.* | | *Phons* |
|---|---|---|---|---|---|---|
| 1,000 | 20 | = | 20 | 40 | = | 40 |
| 500 | 20 | = | 22 | 40 | = | 46 |
| 200 | 20 | = | 25 | 40 | = | 56 |
| 100 | 20 | = | 30 | 40 | = | 72 |
| 50 | 20 | = | 40 | 40 | = | 90 |
| 30 | 20 | = | 60 | 40 | = | 105 |

The above table shows that a note starting at 1,000 cycles at 20 db. above threshold of hearing, and dropping to 30 cycles, would have to be increased in power by 40db. to avoid sounding less loud at 30 cycles.

The above relationship is shown in the form of graphs in Fig. 9a. When a 100 cycle note is increased in intensity from 20 to 40 db., the loudness goes up from 30 to 70 phons. This explains why increase of loudspeaker volume increases the bass out of proportion to middle and upper registers, and often results in boom if carried to excess.

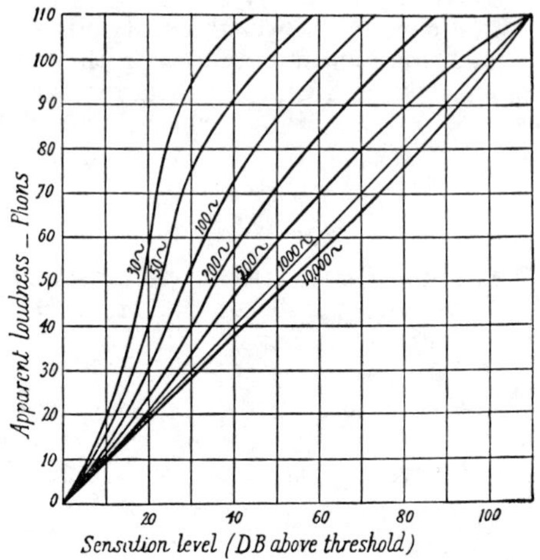


FIG. 9A—Curves to show apparent loudness compared with intensity for various frequencies.

*From Olson and Massa's Applied Acoustics*

## DECIBEL TABLE

The relation between Decibels and Power and Current or Voltage ratios.

| *Power Ratio* | *Decibels* | *Current or Voltage Ratio* | *Decibels* |
|---|---|---|---|
| 1 | 0 | 1 | 0 |
| 2 | 3.0 | 2 | 6.0 |
| 3 | 4.8 | 3 | 9.5 |
| 4 | 6.0 | 4 | 12.0 |
| 5 | 7.0 | 5 | 14.0 |
| 6 | 7.8 | 6 | 15.6 |
| 7 | 8.5 | 7 | 16.9 |
| 8 | 9.0 | 8 | 18.1 |
| 9 | 9.5 | 9 | 19.1 |
| 10 | 10 | 10 | 20 |
| 100 | 20 | 100 | 40 |
| 1,000 | 30 | 1,000 | 60 |
| 10,000 | 40 | 10,000 | 80 |
| 100,000 | 50 | 100,000 | 100 |
| 1,000,000 | 60 | 1,000,000 | 120 |

CHAPTER IX

# FREQUENCY RESPONSE

Music consists of four elements—

*a.* Pitch or Frequency.
*b.* Intensity or Loudness.
*c.* Time or Rhythm.
*d.* Tone quality or Timbre.

It will be clear that a loudspeaker only seriously affects the last of these. It cannot change the pitch of music (apart from introducing one note bass, which only occurs today in poor equipment). Mutilation of the intensity may occur during transmission or recording, when loud passages are subdued to avoid overload and soft passages are strengthened to maintain audibility ; the loudspeaker is blameless in this respect. It certainly does not alter the time or

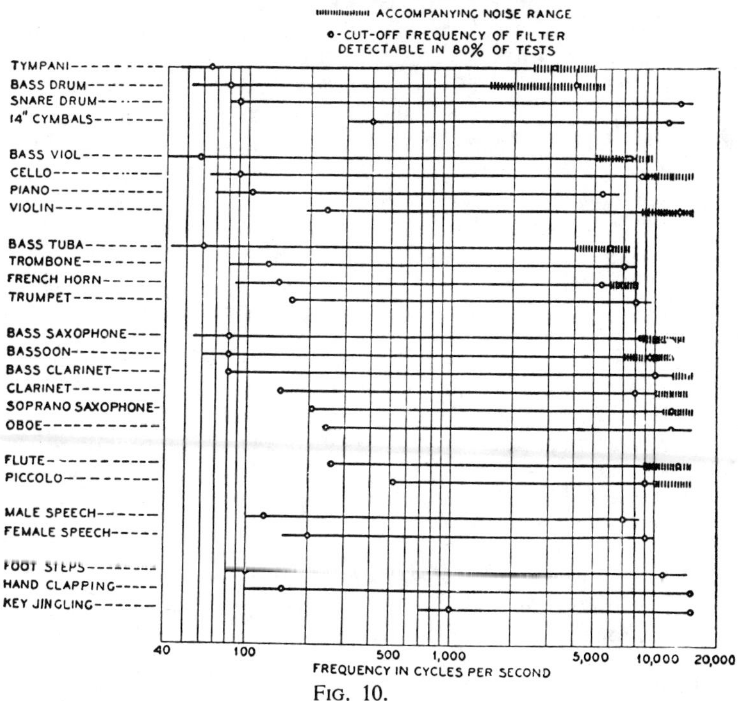


FIG. 10.

*From Seashore's Psychology of Music (McGraw-Hill)*

rhythm of music, so we are left with tone quality or timbre, and this is most certainly seriously affected by the frequency response of the loudspeaker.

The maximum frequency range of the human ear is stated by some authorities to be 20 to 20,000 cycles, although in the tests I have made on young people I have found a cut off at 16,000 cycles. Ability to hear high frequencies recedes with advancing years, and most people over 60 do not hear much above 10,000 cycles, in spite of the fact that they may show no trace of ordinary deafness.

When we consider the frequency range necessary for the reproduction of music, we cannot confine ourselves simply to the frequency of the note being played ; the overtones, the noises associated with the instruments and the relative unimportance of many fundamental frequencies must be taken into account.

Interesting tests were made in America by Snow in 1931, and the results are shown in Fig. 10. It will be noticed that the double bass requires the lowest fundamental of 40 cycles for perfect fidelity and the piano was found to be the only instrument which did not require fundamentals below 100 cycles for true reproduction.

At the upper end of the scale, a cut off at 6,000 cycles did not impair the quality of piano tone, but snare drums, cymbals and the oboe require response well over 10,000 cycles. Hand clapping and key jingling also call for the highest frequencies. Normal listening tests seem to confirm these findings.

It is clear that for laboratory and monitoring work a range of 40 to 16,000 cycles is necessary, but for home listening under present conditions, 40 to 10,000 without serious loss or peaks should be adequate. We still have to contend with needle scratch, whistles and valve hiss, and a reproducer which is too good in the extreme top can, at times, be rather a nuisance. One hesitates to be too dogmatic on this subject, but there is not much doubt that a loudspeaker free from peaks in the 3,000 to 5,000 region and with a falling characteristic from 8,000 to 16,000 cycles, is to be preferred to one with fuller output above 8,000 achieved by prominence in the upper middle register.

## HARMONIC ANALYSIS

At this point it may be of interest to see what actually constitutes a musical tone as heard by the ear. This is found out by harmonic

Author's Note - August 1949.—The above tests by Snow are now rather out-dated. Today, true reproduction of the piano would require a wider range than 100—6000 cycles. Laboratory work would certainly call for L.F. response down to 30 c.p.s. without frequency doubling.

TABLE I. COMPARISON OF PERCENTAGE OF ENERGY AND DECIBEL VALUE IN ONE WAVE OF A VIOLIN TONE, 196~, FURNISHING DATA FOR FIGS. 1, 2a, AND 2b.*

| *Frequency* | *Number of partials* | *Percentage of energy* | *Decibel value* |
|---|---|---|---|
| 196 | 1 | 0.1 | |
| 392 | 2 | 26.0 | 24.2 |
| 588 | 3 | 45.2 | 26.6 |
| 784 | 4 | 8.8 | 19.5 |
| 980 | 5 | 8.5 | 19.3 |
| 1176 | 6 | 4.5 | 16.5 |
| 1372 | 7 | 0.1 | 1.3 |
| 1568 | 8 | 4.8 | 16.8 |
| 1764 | 9 | 0.1 | 0.6 |
| 1960 | 10 | 0.0 | * |
| 2156 | 11 | 0.1 | 1.3 |
| 2352 | 12 | 0.0 | * |
| 2548 | 13 | 0.2 | 2.4 |
| 2744 | 14 | 0.0 | * |
| 2940 | 15 | 0.1 | * |
| 3136 | 16 | 0.0 | * |
| 3332 | 17 | 1.1 | 10.4 |
| 3528 | 18 | 0.1 | * |
| 3724 | 19 | 0.2 | 2.6 |
| 3920 | 20 | 0.0 | |
| | | 99.9 | |

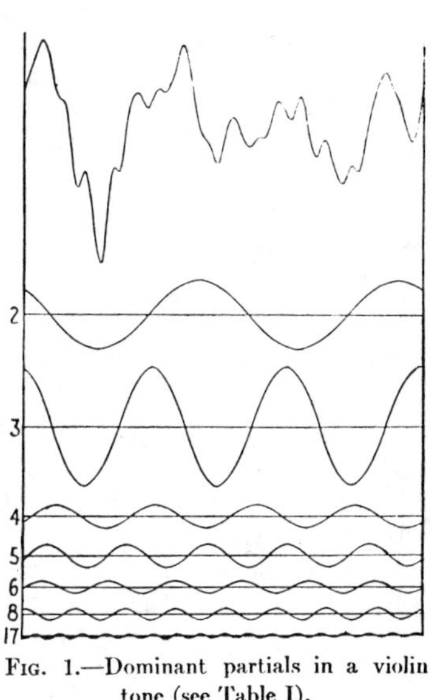


FIG. 1.—Dominant partials in a violin tone (see Table I).

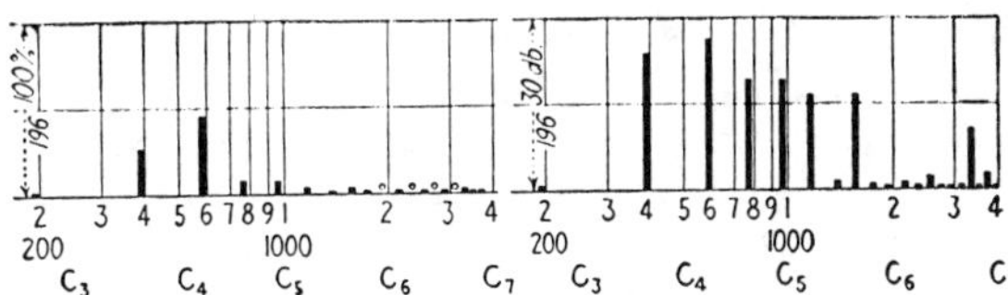


FIG. 2a.—Tone spectrum in terms of percentage of energy.

FIG. 2b.—Tone spectrum in terms of decibel values.

FIG. 11.—Harmonic Analysis.

*From Seashore's Psychology of Music (McGraw-Hill)*

analysis, and an example from Seashore's Psychology of Music, Fig. 11, gives the tone spectrum of the open G string of a violin played with medium intensity. It will be noticed that there is only 0.1% of energy in the fundamental frequency of G 196, and this shows why the fundamental can be omitted from reproduction without destroying the pitch of the note. This fundamental is established by the difference-tone of 196 which occurs between the overtones.

The top wave of Fig 1 is an oscillogram of the full tone, which was analysed up to 20 partials, covering a total frequency range of about four octaves. When one reflects that a single note has such a complicated structure, it is difficult to imagine the thousands of wave formations produced by a full orchestra, and it is astonishing that a loudspeaker cone sorts them out so well as it does. The percentage of energy shows how important are the overtones for true tone colour, and it explains why the violin begins to sound like a flute when severe top cut occurs. The flute is an instrument with most of the energy in the fundamental, especially at low volume.

## TONAL BALANCE

The question of balance is always most important, and affects the listener even more than range. If one end of the scale is cut, it is necessary to cut the other end to balance. A small unit with full input in the top and no bass sounds strident, and is improved by cutting the top to make up for the absence of masking effect from the bass. On the other hand, good bass reproduction without adequate top sounds boomy ; this can be observed in many radio-grams fitted with superhets originally designed as table sets. In such cases results are improved by reducing the bass. The fact is that the human ear can tolerate frequency loss at both ends of the audio range, but is distressed by undue prominence in any section.

It is a good plan to take 800 cycles as a centre point and balance the frequency range above and below it. Thus a commercial set which cuts off seriously at 5,000 cycles should start to fall off at 100 cycles downwards.

This chapter is concluded by a chart showing the piano keyboard with the frequency of each note based on 256 for middle C (although concert pitch today is A439 in Europe, and A440 in America). The wavelength of various notes is given, and any others are easily found by dividing the frequency into 1,120, which is the speed of sound in air in feet per second. Minimum baffle sizes for full bass radiation and 6db. loss are also given.

---

A loudspeaker falls off in bass response at the rate of 6 db per octave below minimum baffle or cabinet area, and at 12 db per octave below frequency of cone resonance.

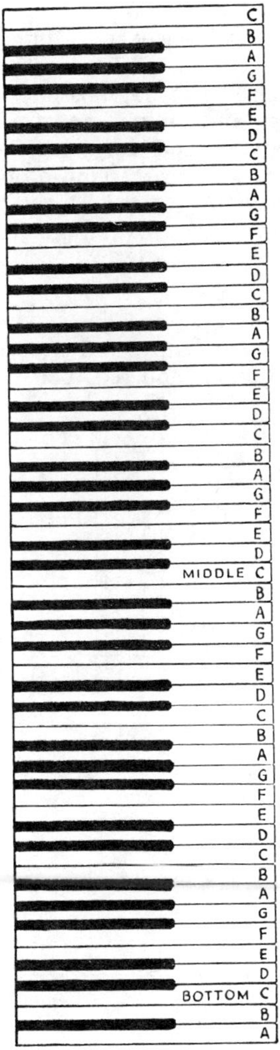

| Key | Frequency C.P.S. | Approx Wave Length | Baffle Area (Diam. in Feet) For Full Radiation | Baffle Area (Diam. in Feet) —6 DB |
|---|---|---|---|---|
| C | 4096 | | | |
| B | 3840 | | | |
| A | 3413 | 3·75" | | |
| G | 3072 | | | |
| F | 2731 | | | |
| E | 2560 | | | |
| D | 2304 | | | |
| C | 2048 | | | |
| B | 1920 | | | |
| A | 1707 | 7·5" | | |
| G | 1536 | | | |
| F | 1365 | | | |
| E | 1280 | | | |
| D | 1152 | | | |
| C | 1024 | | | |
| B | 960 | | | |
| A | 853 | 1'3" | | |
| G | 768 | | | |
| F | 683 | | | |
| E | 640 | | | |
| D | 576 | | | |
| C | 512 | | | |
| B | 480 | | | |
| A | 427 | 2'6" | | |
| G | 384 | | | |
| F | 341 | | | |
| E | 320 | 3'6" | | |
| D | 288 | | | |
| MIDDLE C | 256 | | | |
| B | 240 | | | |
| A | 213 | 5' | 2·5 | |
| G | 192 | | | |
| F | 171 | | | |
| E | 160 | 7' | 3·5 | |
| D | 144 | | | |
| C | 128 | | | |
| B | 120 | | | |
| A | 107 | 10' | 5 | 2·5 |
| G | 96 | | | |
| F | 85 | | | |
| E | 80 | 14' | 7 | 3·5 |
| D | 72 | | | |
| C | 64 | | | |
| B | 60 | | | |
| A | 53 | 20' | 10 | 5 |
| G | 48 | | | |
| F | 43 | | | |
| E | 40 | 28' | 14 | 7 |
| D | 36 | | | |
| BOTTOM C | 32 | 35' | 17 | 8·5 |
| B | 30 | | | |
| A | 27 | 40' | 20 | 10 |

FIG. 12.—Piano Chart.

Approximate length of Open Organ Pipes.

| Frequency | 16 | 32 | 64 | 128 | 256 | c.p.s. |
|---|---|---|---|---|---|---|
| Open Pipe | 32ft. | 16ft. | 8ft. | 4ft. | 2ft. | long. |

The length of a pipe closed at one end is half the above.

CHAPTER X

# RESPONSE CURVES

Although Response Curves vary enormously according to the conditions under which they are taken, they are invaluable for purposes of comparison and research. It is not possible to take these curves in an ordinary room because of reflected waves. It is necessary to go outside away from noise and clear of buildings—preferably in the middle of a field—or construct a sound-proof room acoustically dead. A dead room is one in which all sound waves are absorbed by the walls, floor and ceiling so that no reflection occurs at any frequency. Such a room is costly to construct and difficult to achieve on account of standing waves.

The speaker under test is fed from a low impedance source with the output from an audio frequency oscillator, and its output is picked up by a microphone, then amplified and recorded.

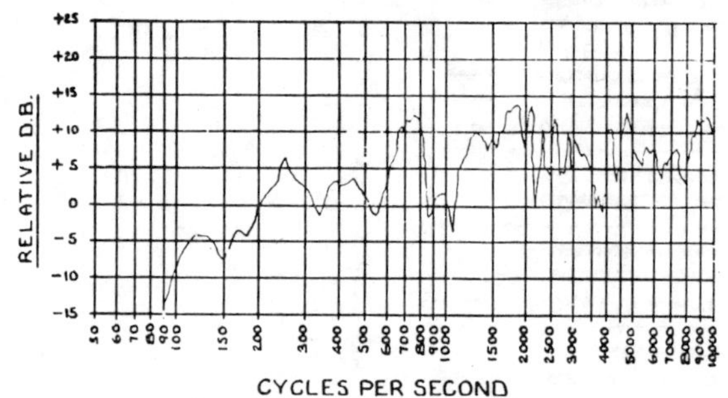


FIG. 13.

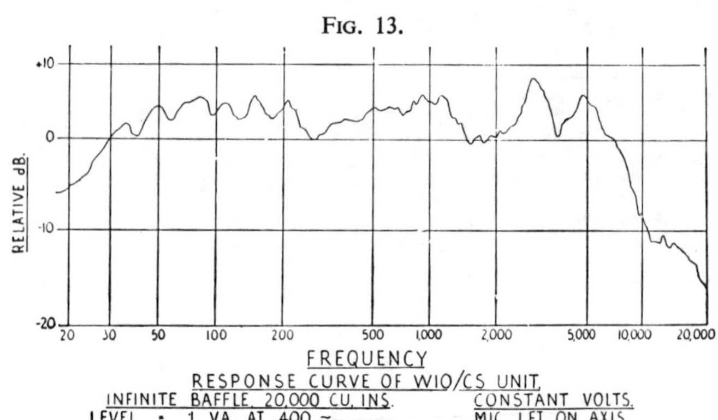


**FIG. 14—10″ Unit with cloth suspension.**

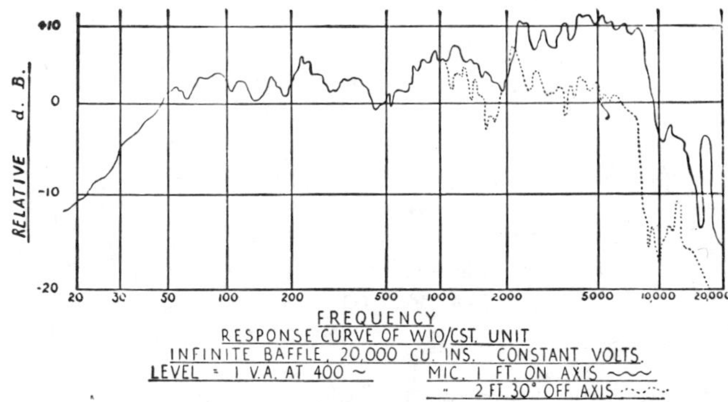


FIG. 15.—10″ Unit—Curved cone with cloth suspension.

Three examples of response curves are given in Figs. 13, 14 and 15. The severe drop in the bass with the 3½″ unit is shown, with a peak at 250 cycles where the fundamental cone resonance occurs.

The two following curves show the increase in high frequency output resulting from the use of a curved cone, compared with a straight-sided cone, with the addition of an extra characteristic to show the drop in output which takes place 30° off axis.

It is usual to assume that a level response under test conditions is the ideal to be aimed at, but in view of the varying effect of room reverberation at different frequencies, this assumption is open to question. In the 1937/38 infinite baffle speaker designed by two members of the Post Office staff, rising characteristic in the treble was specified to balance room absorption of carpets, curtains, cushions, etc., but low notes are also absorbed and are affected by radiation impedance due to size and shape of room. The final test is still a listening test under actual conditions.

Response curves are also useful in exposing the effects of faulty design or construction. See Chapter V, Fig. 4 for effect of unequal pressure around the periphery due to cone being pushed outwards by wrong elevation of centring device.

The main weakness of a response curve is that it does not expose the transient response of the speaker. When a sharp pulse or square wave impulse is fed into a loudspeaker, the transient position is quickly exposed, and any speaker with a mechanical compliance, such as rubber, in the speech coil system, or a joint in the body of the cone, fails to respond sharply to such impulses. The integral cone and coil assembly, with very soft suspension at the periphery of the cone, gives the best results.

## CHAPTER XI

# VOLUME AND WATTS

Many people are puzzled by the rating of loudspeakers in watts. This rating generally refers to the peak input, as the volume — or wattage—is constantly changing. It does not mean that a unit rated at 15 watts is not suitable for 5 watts, although it would be uneconomical to buy a speaker rated far above its probable maximum load, and better results may be possible with a smaller unit.

One watt is the power required to raise a weight of 1 lb. steadily by about 8½ inches per second. Some interesting comparisons are given in "Physics of Music" by A. Wood. For instance a man doing manual labour develops a power of about 100 watts, or enough power to keep alight a 100 watt electric lamp.

We refer, of course, to the power going into the loudspeaker, which is vastly different from the power produced as sound. If the efficiency is 5%, an input of 5 watts will radiate 0.25 watt as actual sound, but heavy losses are common to all musical instruments. To quote again from "Physics of Music", a large organ may require an engine developing 10 kilowatts (10,000 watts) to blow it, yet all that appears as sound may be 12-14 watts. A pianist may use energy at the rate of 200 watts to produce 0.4 watt as sound. The human voice is a most efficient musical transformer, yet only 1% of the energy used by a vocalist goes to charm the audience, (all from "Physics of Music").

It is customary to complain about the inefficiency of the loudspeaker in transforming energy into sound, but in comparison with other musical transformers it comes out very well, and the usual minimum 2% calculation appears to be satisfactory, while a figure of 30% efficiency for exponential horns at certain frequencies is remarkably good. The average power radiated by a violin would be about .002 watt. With a speaker efficiency of 2% this requires only one-tenth of a watt input. As the frequency range of a violin is 200 to 9,000 cycles (including overtones) very good reproduction is possible with a small set and a small speaker.

Now the piano radiates about 0.4 watt, with a frequency range of 70 to 7,000 cycles for good reproduction, so the small speaker with its assumed efficiency of 2% would require 20 watts for full reproduction, which is obviously impracticable. In any case, most of the power is used in the bass, so we must turn to a larger unit, adequately baffled, for full scale results. Take a 10″ speaker with about 10,000 lines flux density. Here the efficiency may be about 5%, requiring 8 watts input at full volume, which sounds a more reasonable proposition. If we now improve efficiency still more by using a bass reflex cabinet, and an extra speaker for treble, reflect the top, and use better magnets, we may get an efficiency of 10/15% and reduce the required input to 4 watts or less. The nett result is that we reduce the dangers of overloading both the set and the speaker, and we completely alter the balance of power between treble and bass. In the case of the small unit any attempt to approach full volume would result in distortion and distressing overload. In the second case, a 10 watt amplifier would provide the required input for the 10″ unit, but bass resonance would probably be excessive. In the third case, full piano range and volume are available from 5 watt equipment, the treble is not stressed, and results are "easy on the ears". No doubt such a set-up would cure the habit of the average listener of turning the tone control to "mellow", which is partly due to unbalanced power in the frequency range of the reproduction.

We have taken the piano to illustrate the question of watts and loudspeaker balance, because we all realise easily what is meant by full piano volume. The same arguments apply to the orchestra, with much greater force.

For domestic use, an output of 5 watts with not more than 0.1% distortion should satisfy the most critical listener. For those who like to blow the roof off occasionally when the rest of the family is out of ear-shot, a 10 watt job is ideal. It should be understood that 10 watts undistorted output is more tolerable than 5 watts with 2% distortion.

## PEAK INPUT

It is advisable to observe the input limits stipulated by speaker makers. Occasional overload does not matter, but continuous overload leads to trouble.

The main causes of overload in a speaker are the following—

1. Excessive heat generated in the speech coil.
2. Excessive movement of the speech coil in and out of the magnetic gap.
3. Actual distortion of the cone shape or walls.
4. Distortion due to suspension.

Let us examine these effects in turn—

1. Excessive heat is the most serious danger because it can occur without audible warning, and eventually leads to breakdown of insulation or adhesives, or to distortion in the shape of the coil.

Movement of the coil on low notes helps to reduce temperature, so it follows that a speaker used only for treble reproduction is more prone to over-heating than when used also for bass. A large diameter coil will naturally carry more current than a smaller one, as thicker wire can be used for the required resistance.

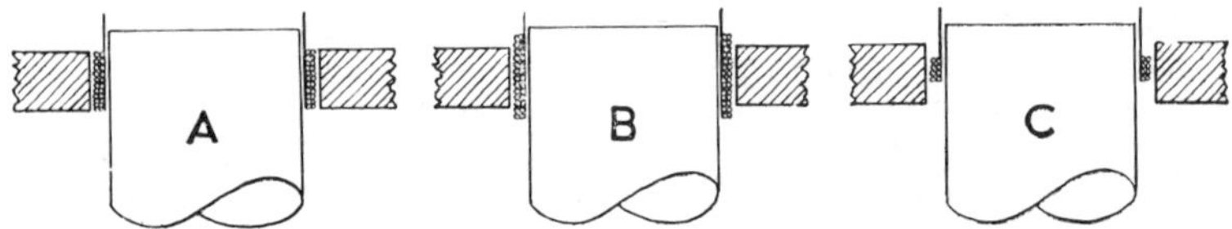


FIG. 16—Variations of speech coil length, to counter large L.F. movements.

2. Excessive movement of the coil in and out of the gap causes harmonic distortion, due to variation in the flux cut by the coil. Non-linear distortion of this type can be reduced by making the coil shorter than the gap so that it remains in a uniform field, or by lengthening the coil so that one side moves in to a stronger field as the other side moves into a weaker one. Either of these arrangements leads to loss of efficiency if carried to excess. A speaker with the desirable attribute of free suspension is more prone to distortion of this sort than one with stiff suspension, and is therefore usually rated lower in watts. Distortion resulting from this form of overloading should be eliminated by reducing the volume, or by using two speakers and separator.

3. Actual overloading of the cone is not very common in these days and it is surprising how much punishment a well-made cone will absorb without complaint. The straight-sided cone is better than a curved or so-called exponential cone in this respect. Much of the distortion commonly attributed to the speaker is due to amplifier overload.

4. Suspension. In practically all loudspeakers, the stiffness of the suspension increases with amplitude, and distortion (mostly third harmonic) occurs in the bass, particularly below the resonance point, if the movement and volume are excessive. There is not much the user can do about this, apart from improving the loading by acoustic chambers, or using two speakers (see Chapters on Impedance and Cabinets)

## CHAPTER XII

# RESONANCE AND VIBRATION

Sound consists of two sorts of vibration—forced and free. The definitions by A. Wood in "Physics of Music" are as follows—

Free Vibration. Any source of sound if set in vibration and left to itself vibrates in its own natural frequency, producing a note which gradually dies away as the vibrations decrease, but remains constant in pitch. This type of vibration is called free vibration.

Forced Vibration. If a force which varies periodically is applied to a vibrating system, the system vibrates in the period of the force with an amplitude which is generally small. This is forced vibration.

The response of a vibrating system when subjected to a force timed to its own period is called RESONANCE. This resonance is the particular case of forced vibrations when the force and the system are in unison.

Musical instruments are examples of forced and free vibrations. In the piano, the string provides the forced vibrations to which the sound-board responds. In a loudspeaker, the cone assembly responds to forced vibrations, but free vibration occurs at the natural frequency of the cone (and to a smaller degree of the centring device). These are RESONANCES. Acoustic and Reflex Cabinets also act as vibrating systems, with free vibration or resonance at a natural frequency depending on the volume and length of air column.

In the case of the piano, the vibrating string must impose its frequency on the sound-board without the frequency of the string being in any way modified by the sound-board (A. Wood). In the same way, the forced vibrations of the loudspeaker must not be unduly affected by the free vibrations or resonance. It is equally important to subdue or control all vibrations, whether forced or free, arising in the cabinet system, which is in fact a continuation of the loudspeaker system used for coupling the sound waves to the room.

In a freely vibrating string, other modes of vibration occur in addition to the fundamental, the frequencies being 2, 3, 4 or more times the fundamental. These are known as second, third, etc. harmonics and are shown in Fig. 17.

The relative strength of the overtones decides the tone quality of the note, and maximum resonance is looked for in a musical instrument, which the loudspeaker is expected to reproduce as forced vibrations.

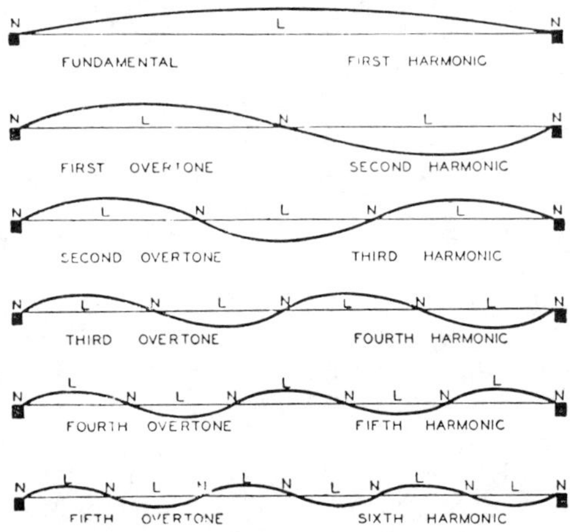


FIG. 17—Modes of vibration of a stretched string.
N.—The points of rest are termed nodes.
L.—The points of maximum amplitude are termed antinodes or loops.

*From Olson's Elements of Acoustical Engineering*

## BASS RESONANCE

Now the free vibration or bass resonance of a loudspeaker depends on the weight and suspension stiffness of the cone and centring device. Anything above 80 cycles is too high for reasonably good quality, and open baffle resonance below 30 cycles gives rather thin bass when accompanied by wide response in the treble, at domestic volume levels. On the other hand, when a 15-inch speaker with open baffle resonance about 25/30 cycles is given reflex loading of adequate cubic volume and rigidity, the cone resonance drops to 15 or 18 cycles and the all-important air-column resonance can be held down to below 55 cycles. This results in reproduction of speech free from colouration (assuming, of course, suitable high-frequency speaker with crossover network) and bass response in musical items which is deep and crisp.

## CABINET RESONANCE

We now come to the kind of resonance with which we are all familiar—generally described as cabinet resonance. The following remarks apply mainly to ordinary cabinets, as it is assumed that Reflex and Labyrinth types will have received special consideration.

There are three main types of Cabinet resonance—

*a*. Vibration of the cabinet itself.
*b*. Vibration of the air inside the cabinet.
*c*. Vibration of the cabinet back.

Of these, the *b* type is the worst and is the most difficult to control.

### (*a*) VIBRATION OF CABINET

Actual cabinet resonance may not be very prevalent at low volume, but is intensified as the volume level is increased. Bakelite of thin cross-section may give offence to the ear but is satisfactory if its cross-section is adequate for the size of the cabinet. Acoustically, there is a wide choice of material, provided it is thick enough. Wood, bakelite, steel, asbestos, clay, fibre, plaster, cement, bricks and mortar, even cardboard could be successfully employed. Naturally, the necessary thickness varies, and ⅛″ steel would be far better than ½″ cardboard. (See absorption coefficients of materials, Fig 30, in Chapter XVI.).

(I recently heard a large corner cabinet moulded in clay and fired. Fitted with two speakers and cross-over unit, the whole outfit weighed nearly 200 lbs., but results were very good). As a matter of fact, weight gives a good indication of the merit of cabinet material—the heavier the better.

### (*b*) AIR RESONANCE

As this depends on the size and shape of the cabinet, it is not always easy to control without a major operation. The worst effects are generally due to the cabinet sides being too wide for the frontal area. Improvement may be effected by mounting the speaker further back in the cabinet, or by spacing the unit ⅛″ or more away from its baffle, thus relieving the air pressure around the edge of the cone. Lining a cabinet with felt absorbs middle and upper frequencies more than bass.

Placing thick wooden reflectors along two or three sides of the speaker, 6″ or 8″ in depth, may lower the cone resonance and subdue pressure points in the cabinet.

Wrapping the speaker unit in a cotton bag reduces the amplitude of the fundamental resonance. Probably the best cure for boomy reproduction is to connect another speaker in parallel. This cuts down the voltage at resonance, (see Fig. 22.) and if the extra speaker has good H.F. response and is correctly phased and placed immediately above the existing cabinet *in the same plane*, the improvement is phenomenal. An efficient 5/6″ unit in small open back cabinet does well here.

### (*c*) CABINET BACKS

If the cabinet or baffle is fitted with a cardboard back which vibrates, it is intensifying certain frequencies and causing distortion. It should be removed.

## CHAPTER XIII

# CABINETS AND BAFFLES

The cabinet or baffle should be looked upon as a means of coupling the vibrations of the cone to the air, rather than as a piece of furniture for housing or mounting the loudspeaker. Actually, the loudspeaker is a transducer which takes over energy from the set or amplifier in the form of A.C. current and terminates in the form of sound waves absorbed by the boundaries of the room. Unfortunately most of this energy is wasted in the form of heat, and the object of this chapter is to consider methods of avoiding this loss as much as possible ; in other words, to consider efficiency of coupling between loudspeaker and room.

Small baffles and cabinets are convenient in use, but are inefficient and introduce distortion. The following diagram from "Radio Engineering Handbook" gives an estimate of distortion at low frequencies from the ordinary open back console cabinet.

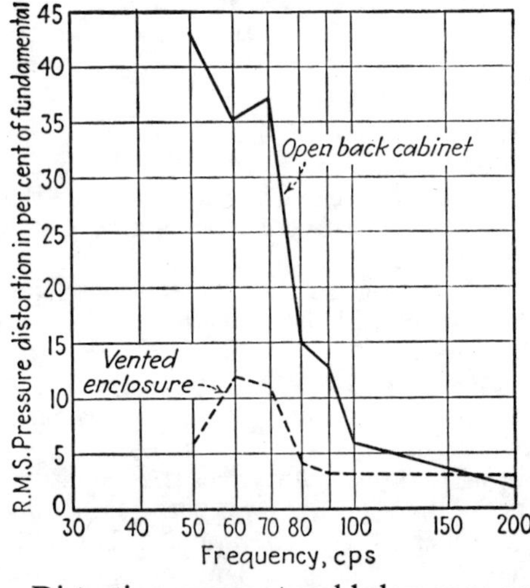


It should be understood that all references to open back Cabinets include such Cabinets fitted with perforated cardboard or plywood backs. Cabinet distortion is usually intensified by this type of back.

FIG.18. - Comparison between open back cabinet and vented enclosure of same size.
(*Henney*)

Distortion occurs at and below cone resonance.

There is uneven response from the open back cabinet due to increased output in the region 100 to 500 cycles from pressure points, and severe loss of bass, according to size of cabinet, plus frequency doubling. Similar results occur with small baffles, especially when fitted with cardboard backs.

There are many ways of mounting a loudspeaker apart from the ordinary cabinet. The main systems are—

*a.* Infinite baffle.
*b.* Large open baffle.
*c.* Large open back cabinet.
*d.* Reflex cabinet.
*e.* Acoustic labyrinth.
*f.* Exponential horn.

Let us consider the merits and drawbacks of each system in turn.

## (*a*) INFINITE BAFFLE

Acoustically this appears to offer the nearest approach to perfection. A true infinite baffle is achieved by mounting the unit in the wall of the room, so that loading is approximately equal on each side of the cone. there is full bass radiation down to resonance of cone, there is an entire absence of cabinet and air column resonance and the radiation impedance seen by the cone is very good. Various methods of mounting are shown in Room Acoustics. (Chapter XVI, Fig. 29).

The efficiency in one room is not so good as a Reflex Cabinet and there may be inconvenience in the radiation which occurs from the back of the speaker. So-called infinite baffles consisting of a totally enclosed box should not be mistaken for a true infinite baffle. Such a box, unless of adequate size, imposes undue pressure on the cone which actually raises the resonant frequency and mars the reproduction of music. (An open free-edge cone would be an exception.)

The absence of resonance above the fundamental is shown in the following curve, Fig. 19/B, which represents two speakers

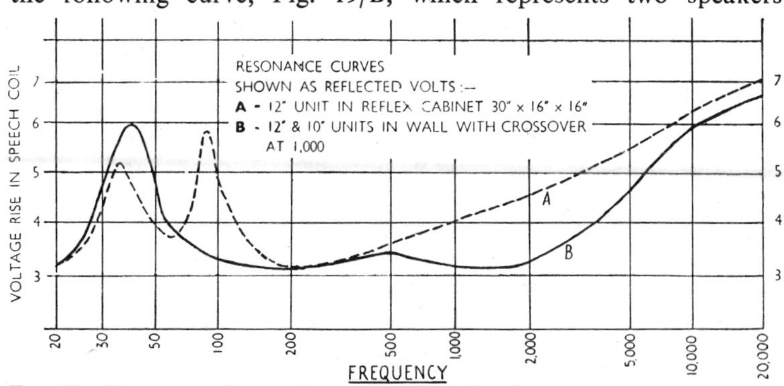


Fig. 19—Resonance Curves shown as reflected volts.
A. 12″ Unit in Reflex Cabinet, 30″ × 16″ × 16″.
B. 12″ and 10″ Units in Wall with Crossover at 1,000 cycles

mounted in the wall of a room with a cross-over at 1,000 cycles, compared with one 12″ speaker in Reflex cabinet 30″ × 16″ × 16″. Incidentally, reflected volts give quite a good picture of the degree of resonance including spurious vibration such as loose mesh, thin panels, etc.

Curve A shows the main cone resonance at 35 cycles, with the more pronounced air-column resonance at 90 due to cabinet.

### (*b*) LARGE OPEN BAFFLE

If we accept the premise that the true infinite baffle is the best system, then it follows that the nearer we approach the arrangement the better the results will be. An open baffle therefore should be as big as possible, and the wavelength chart in Chapter IX, Fig. 12 gives various sizes for various rates of cut-off. The diameter of a baffle should be at least half the wavelength of the lowest frequency required at full power. Below this size, efficiency falls off at the rate of 6 db. per octave. Thus a 5-ft baffle starts to cut off at 110 cycles and a 7½-ft. baffle at 75 cycles. All baffle resonance should be eliminated by using substantial material. Solid wood one inch thick, ¾″ plywood, ⅜″ asbestos, or any similar materials, are satisfactory. A corner position improves radiation resistance and angle seen by the cone. A large baffle gives very good results.

### (*c*) LARGE OPEN BACK CABINET

The conditions here are similar to a large baffle and should be as good, provided the sides are not deep in relation to frontal area, and the interior of the cabinet is not filled with equipment. Baffle area is increased by width of sides.

### (*d*) PHASE INVERSION OR REFLEX CABINET

This arrangement seems to offer the easiest solution to the problem of obtaining large-scale results with reasonable dimensions. Construction and design are simple, and good results are possible within fairly wide limits. The fundamental cone resonance can be lowered by almost an octave with the best size of port and cabinet.

The improved bass response may result in a very deep tone unless a loudspeaker with good top response is used. A high note speaker may be added, preferably with cross-over at about 1,000 cycles, to balance the increased low note radiation.

Tests have been made with various sizes of speaker and cabinet, and Fig. 20 gives a general outline of the cabinets used. It was found that variations of 2 or 3 inches in the size of cabinet do not seriously affect results, and the dominating factor is the cone resonance of the unit, which also controls the frequency of the all-important air-column resonance. Increasing the length of one cabinet from 30 inches to 60 inches only resulted in a rise of 5 cycles in the cone resonance and a drop of 7 cycles in the air-column resonance, although the free resonance had actually gone down from 110 to 83. Another interesting point is that fitting an internal reflector does not actually lengthen the air-column, so far as the resonance is concerned[1] Closing the port usually lumps both cone and air-column resonances together at a fairly high frequency, due to heavy damping on the cone.

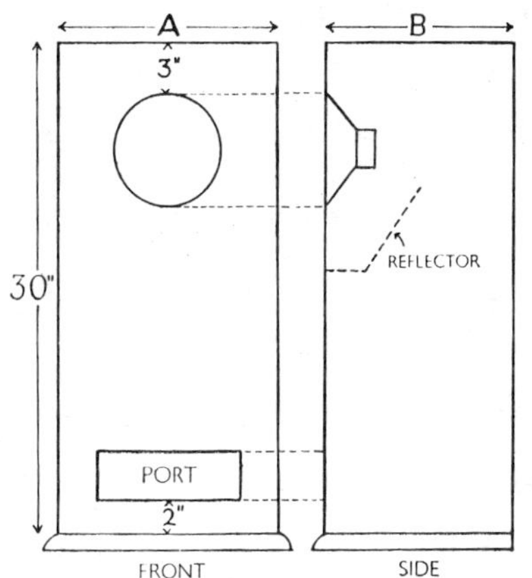


*Minimum Dimensions*

| | *A* | *B* | *Port* |
|---|---|---|---|
| 8″ Unit | 15″ | 8″ | 9″ × 2″ |
| 10″ Unit | 15″ | 12″ | 9″ × 3″ |
| 12″ Unit | 17″ | 12″ | 10″ × 3″ |

1″ Solid Wood or
$\frac{3}{4}$″ Ply Wood
Solid Back.

FIG. 20.—Outline of Reflex Cabinets used in tests. Reflector Optional.

Larger cabinets of more solid construction would give better results.

The following speakers were used throughout—

| | | | |
|---|---|---|---|
| 6″ Unit | 1″ Pole | 8,000 lines | |
| 8″ ,, | 1″ ,, | 10,000 ,, | |
| 10″ ,, | 1″ ,, | 14,000 ,, | (with cloth surround) |
| 12″ ,, | 1$\frac{3}{4}$″ ,, | 13,000 ,, | |

Six different sizes of cabinet were used, all substantially made with air-tight backs, and detailed results now follow. The open baffle resonance of each speaker is given to demonstrate the effect of Reflex loading

An internal reflector affects the phasing, lowers the cone resonance by 3 to 5 cycles by extra damping, but makes no difference to the frequency of the air column resonance.

---

(1) Internal Reflectors are sometimes referred to as folded pipes.

# REFLEX CABINET TESTS

| *Ref.* | *Size of Cabinet* | *Apprx. Cu. Feet* | *Apprx. Length of Air Col'n* | *Unit* | *Open Baffle* | MAIN RESONANCES *Port Open* | *Port Closed* |
|---|---|---|---|---|---|---|---|
| A | 15″ × 12″ × 6″ | 0.6 | 1 ft. | 8″ | 70 | Cone 75<br>Air Col. 170 | } 150 |
| B1 | 30″ × 15″ × 8″ | 2 | 2½ ft. | 6″ | 160 | Cone 160<br>Air·Col. 110 | } 150 |
| B2 | 30″ × 15″ × 8″ | 2 | 2½ ft. | 8″ | 70 | Cone 45<br>Air. Col. 75 | } 80 |
| C | 60″ × 15″ × 8″ | 4 | 5 ft. | 8″ | 70 | Cone 60<br>Air Col. 83 | 60<br>85 |
| D1 | 30″ × 15″ × 12″ | 3 | 2½ ft. | 8″ | 70 | Cone 50<br>Air Col. 82 | } 80 |
| D2 | 30″ × 15″ × 12″ | 3 | 2½ ft. | 10″ | 57 | Cone 35<br>Air Col. 62 | 58<br>80 |
| E1 | 30″ × 15″ × 15″ R | 3½ | 2½ ft. | 8″ | 70 | Cone 45<br>Air Col. 85 | } 75 |
| E2 | 30″ × 15″ × 15″ R | 3½ | 2½ ft. | 10″ | 57 | Cone 35<br>Air Col. 75 | } 65 |
| F | 30″ × 16″ × 16″ R | 4 | 2½ ft. | 12″ | 60 | Cone 35<br>Air Col. 85 | } 70 |

R—Cabinet fitted with internal Reflector.

A comparative listening test gave the following results—

A. 8″ Unit. Cabinet too small, tone boxy, poor top. Inferior to normal open-back cabinet.

B1. 6″ Unit. Very good results for size of unit. Pure bass at air-column resonance of 110. Superior to usual small cabinet or baffle and much better than A, but cone resonance far too noticeable.

B2 8″ Unit. Very good on music with pure bass. Air resonance affects speech which is improved by closing the port.

C. 8″ Unit in tall experimental cabinet. Very good. Speech better than B2. No reflex effect through port.

D.1. 8″ Unit. Very fine bass. Boomy on speech. Requires separate treble unit for good, all-round results.

D2. 10″ Unit. Excellent quality.

E1. 8″ Unit. Similar to D1, but still deeper tone.

E2 10″ Unit. Similar to D2.

F. 12″ Unit. Very good all-round results, but slight resonance on speech. (See Fig. 19.)

The main characteristics of Reflex Cabinets may be summarised as follows—

1. The cone resonance is lowered, thus reducing the extent of non-linearity in the bass, with much improvement to quality.
2. There is a pronounced cabinet air-column resonance which should be held below 90 cycles, otherwise speech is affected.
3. This air resonance is linear and does not distort music. Its frequency is affected by size and shape of cabinet, size of port, and type of speaker.
4. Starting with a large port area, the cone and air-column resonances are lowered as the size of opening is reduced until the lowest point is reached. Further reduction of opening raises the cone resonance until a sort of infinite baffle is made.
5. Improved loading at low frequencies increases the power handling capacity and extends the response (see Fig. 21)

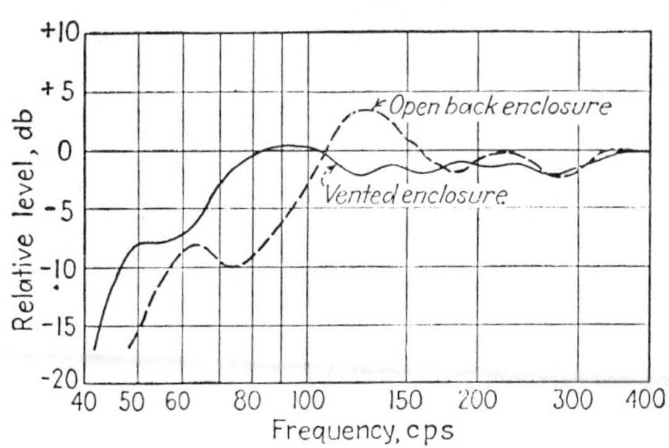


FIG. 21.—Total sound power radiated by cabinet for which distortion is shown in Fig. 18.

***From Henney's Radio Engineering Handbook***

6. The cabinet enclosure behaves like a pipe closed at one end. The first overtone is therefore third harmonic.
7. At low frequency, the port emission is mostly in phase with frontal output of speaker [1] Placing the port near

[1] See Phase effects. Chapter XXIV

the speaker improves the mutual radiation impedance and increases the power. As a rule this is not necessary. The size of the port is not critical, as variations of 1″ or 2″ in diameter have little effect.

8. The back-of-cone radiation in upper registers is mostly lost. Consequently, a cone with strong top response is necessary to preserve tonal balance if an additional unit is not used.

9. A loudspeaker with open baffle resonance above 75 cycles is not considered suitable for Reflex loading.

10. The air-column resonance may be free or forced vibration. (See Chapter XII.). To find the free resonance, insert a small speaker with high cone resonance, and a search with A.F. oscillator will reveal the natural period. In cabinet B this is 110 cycles. When using a larger speaker with low cone resonance, the cone takes charge and brings the air-column resonance down. This is a most important aspect of acoustic loading.

11. Any air leakage around the cabinet back leads to inefficient loading. Perfect sealing may lower both cone and air-column resonances by 10 cycles.

12. Cone resonance, air-column resonance, and cabinet vibrations (if any) are reflected back on the output transformer as a rise in voltage and impedance. Negative feedback, therefore, helps to reduce them.

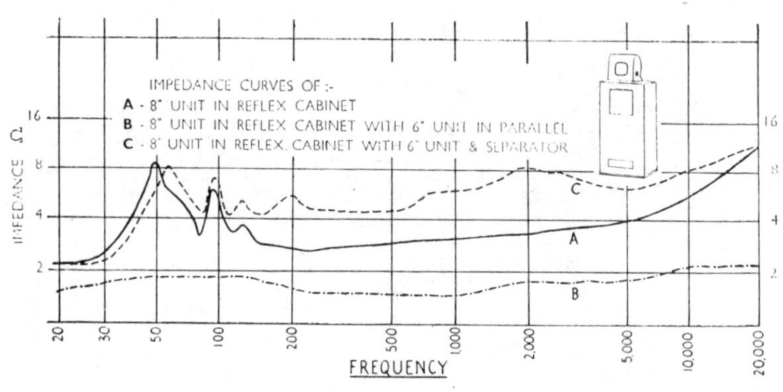


Fig. 22/1.

13. If reproduction is too deep or resonant, one of the following arrangements may be tried—

(*a*) Space the loudspeaker ⅛″ or ¼″ away from cabinet front. Air resonance can be completely relieved. (See Fig. 22/2.)

(*b*) Connect an extra speaker, of different size and resonance, in parallel. This flattens the impedance curve and gives reproduction almost entirely free from resonance. (See Figs. 22/1 and 22/2.)

(*c*) Use extra speaker with separator. This preserves full bass response, with improved "top", free from intermodulation and cabinet distortion. (See Fig. 22/1)

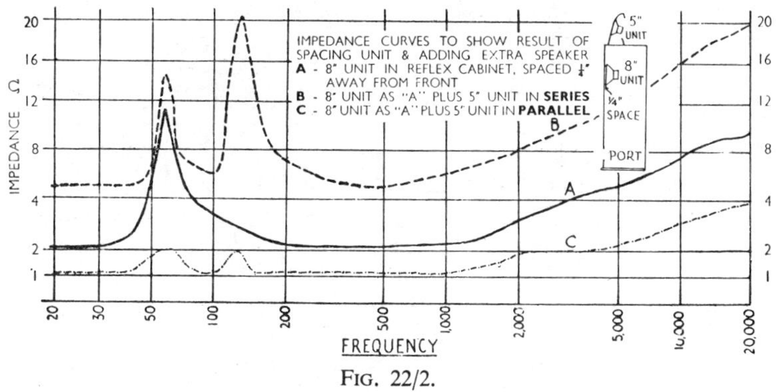


Fig. 22/2.

## (*e*) ACOUSTIC LABYRINTH

This differs from the Reflex Cabinet in two ways : An effort is made to balance the cone or air resonance by making the labyrinth one quarter wavelength. Thus a resonance of 50 cycles equals 22.4 ft., calling for a labyrinth about 5½ ft. long. The distance from a node to the next antinode is always one quarter of a wavelength, and at this point the sound waves are out of phase. The port emission should therefore reduce output from the speaker at resonance. The second point is that the labyrinth must be lined with felt or other material to absorb resonances at middle frequencies from the many reflecting surfaces.

It will be appreciated that the resonance of the speaker cannot be determined until it has been tried in the cabinet, so that production of one balanced labyrinth may involve considerable alterations. Also the frequency of the resonance may go down as the suspension becomes more flexible with use. Even so, very good results may be expected without accurate wavelength matching, as most of the advantages of the Reflex type apply to the labyrinth with equal force. (See Chapter XXIV : Phase effects)

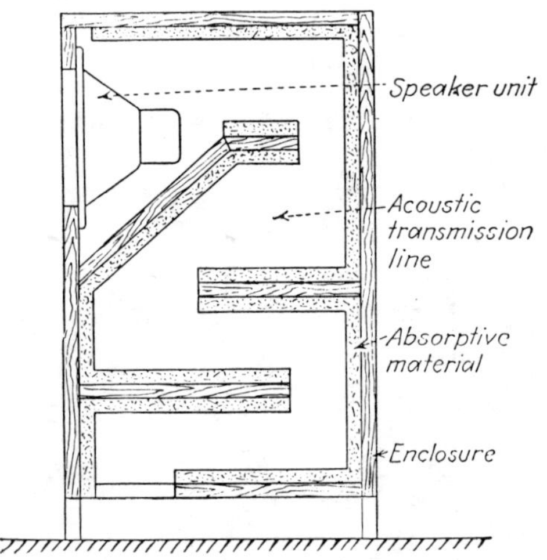


FIG. 23.—Labyrinth type of transmission-line speaker.
*From Henney's Radio Engineering Handbook*

The general conclusion is that the acoustic labyrinth gives better bass than the reflex cabinet, but there is more absorption of the upper middle register. Although the upper register is not reflected through the port, there is an obvious loss due to the lining of the labyrinth.

SPECIAL NOTE—

Fifteen-inch speakers with 8/9 cubic feet of air loading and a port 9″ × 6″, can be designed to give a cone resonance at 18 cycles with air-column resonance at 50 cycles. An extra speaker for top-note reproduction, with separator, is essential, but the combination gives very good results. Bass is strong and crisp, and speech is clear and free from resonance.

The open baffle resonance of the 15″ speaker should not be higher than about 35 c/s. This low resonance may call for cloth suspension to the cone. (See pages 83 and 84 for practical applications of the system).

## (*f*) EXPONENTIAL HORNS

The calculations involved in correct horn loading are far beyond the scope of this little book, and very bad results may be had by hit and miss methods. The subject is exhaustively examined in Olson's *Elements of Acoustical Engineering* (Chapman & Hall), from which the following interesting double-horn arrangement is taken

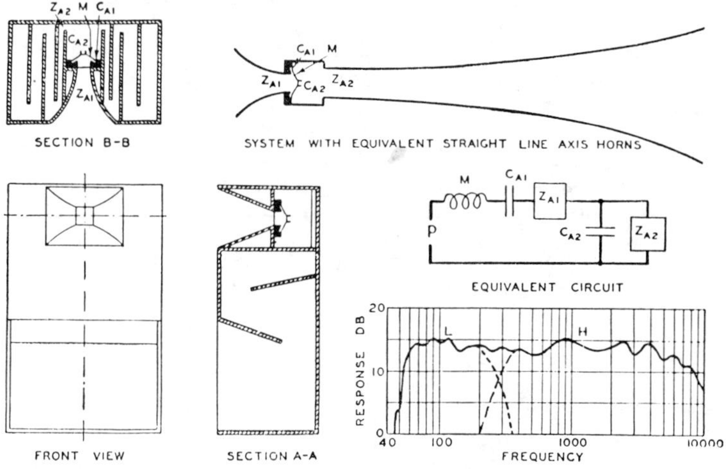


FIG. 24.—Compound Horn Loudspeaker.

*From Olson's Elements of Acoustical Engineering*

An arrangement on the above lines offers interesting possibilities. A combination of small horn for treble and acoustic labyrinth for bass would also be promising, and would be a much simpler proposition.

The efficiency of a horn is limited to a certain frequency range, depending on its shape, length and diameter. A large exponential horn is necessary for low notes, and a short flare for high notes. Each type can be designed to cover 3 to 4 octaves reasonably well, and it is usual to arrange a cross-over at 300 or 400 cycles in order to cope with 8 octaves from 40 to 10,000 cycles.

A flare, 12″ long with a mouth 12″ in diameter will have directional properties as good as a 3″ speaker at high frequencies, but multi-cellular horns (Fig. 26 and 27) are often used to cover a very wide tangle.

For outdoor work and large buildings, where big volume is required, the efficiency of exponential horns results in important economies in amplifier requirements.

## CHAPTER XIV

# EXTENSION SPEAKERS AND VOLUME CONTROLS

These are in such common use that there is no necessity to explain in detail how they work. The simplest way to run an extension speaker is at low impedance, i.e. from secondary of existing output transformer, and practically all new sets are now fitted with speaker points within the 1½ to 5 ohm range. It was always impossible to understand why some set makers provided high impedance extension points, thus forcing the user of an extension speaker to waste money on another transformer, to lose some of his precious top response in the flex and additional transformer, and to receive an electric shock if he touched the extension leads, especially during a loud passage of music. The voltage across the primary of the output transformer of an average domestic radio set may be 300 volts D.C. plus speech voltage of 250 AC. Although not generally lethal, such voltages need not be brought out of a set and circulated around the house to a loudspeaker with bare terminals.

The only possible objection to low impedance runs is loss of power, and this hardly arises under domestic conditions. The average distance between set and extension speaker will be about 30 ft. Using ordinary 14/36 flex, the total resistance for 60 ft. is 0.75 ohms approximately. With a 3 ohm speaker this means that one-third of the power is wasted. Such a drop in volume is barely audible. For longer runs it is advisable to use heavier wire, such as—

| | | | | |
|---|---|---|---|---|
| 23/36 | = | 23/.0076 | Resistance | 0.80 ohms per 100 ft. |
| 20s | = | 1/.036 | ,, | 0.75 ,, ,, ,, ,, |
| 18s | = | 1/.048 | ,, | 0.45 ,, ,, ,, ,, |

A distance of 50 ft. means the resistance of 100 ft. (there and back).

In spite of the rude things which are often said about small sets and speakers, there are plenty of occasions when they are preferable to large ones, such as for kitchen or bedside use. If a kitchen loudspeaker is exposed to steam or vapour it will deteriorate, and it is advisable to wrap the entire cabinet in cellophane. This will keep out the steam without spoiling the appearance of the cabinet, and without undue loss of volume.

The main objection to bedroom extension speakers is the problem of switching the set on and off. A simple remote control which is not often used, is to have fitted the type of two-way switch commonly used for controlling hall and landing lights. Any electrician could run some neat P.V.C. coloured flex to the bedroom switch, and the set could be switched on or off either upstairs or downstairs, without recourse to expensive relay installations.

Many sets are capable of giving better reproduction than is obtained from the speaker mounted in the cabinet, surrounded by wireless components. Special baffles or acoustic cabinets may well be justified. But it is very important to remember that high-fidelity speakers ruthlessly expose any distortion or hum, and may give worse audible results instead of better. If the set speaker has been selected to silence valve hiss, to peak at 4,000 cycles, and to be deaf to mains hum at 50/100 cycles, woe betide your hi-fi efforts !

## VOLUME CONTROLS

There are four main systems of loudspeaker volume control—

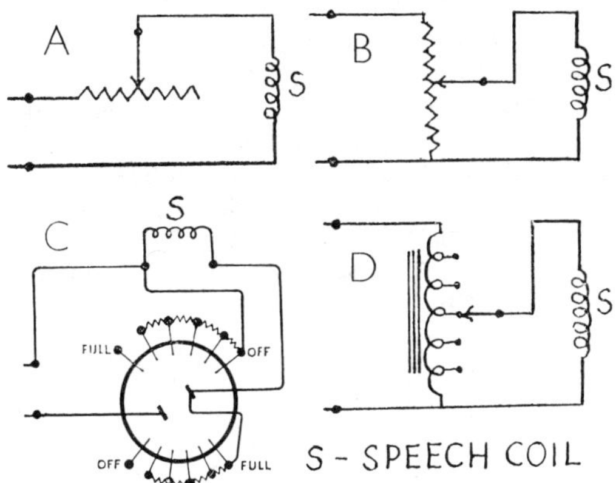


FIG. 25.—Loudspeaker Volume Controls.
A. Variable Resistance. B. Potentiometer.
C. Constant Impedance. D. Tapped Choke

As the impedance of the loudspeaker varies with frequency (see Chapter VII, Fig. 6) its performance may be seriously affected by the volume control ; in some cases the quality is ruined, but in others it may even be improved. Results will be disastrous if the volume control is expected to do an unreasonable amount of work, as it is always advisable to control volume as near the source as possible. It is impossible to reduce 5 watts to one-tenth of a watt in a loudspeaker circuit without distortion.

The variable resistance method A is not used today as it tends to emphasise the bass resonance, and reduce the middle frequencies more than the top. It is also necessary to have a high value of resistance to give effective control. As the resistance is in series with the speech coil, it has a greater effect on the level parts of the impedance curve than it has on the peaks, hence the deterioration in quality.

**Method B.**—The potentiometer is a distinct improvement on Method A, provided the resistance value is kept low. As the potentiometer is permanently connected across the line, the resistance must nevertheless be made high enough to avoid undue loss of power. A value of about 3 times the average impedance of the speaker offers a reasonable compromise, and furnishes a continuously variable control which is quite satisfactory on the average extension speaker.

**Method C.**—Constant Impedance Control. This constitutes a further advance on Method B. The resistances are arranged in series and in parallel with the speech coil so that the total load across the line is the same at any setting of the control, and at full volume no resistance is in circuit at all. The control has the effect of levelling the impedance curve and is well worth consideration for reducing bass resonance, particularly on speech in Reflex Cabinets. This type of control is worked in steps and has not the advantage of being continuously variable.

**Method D.**—Tapped choke or auto transformer. Unlike the three previous types, this control has practically no effect on the frequency response, and may be used with loudspeaker cross-over networks without upsetting the performance. It is obviously much more expensive and bulky. The impedance rises as the volume is reduced, and it should not be used with a high impedance source such as a pentode without negative feed back.

CHAPTER XV

# CINEMA SPEAKERS

The quality of reproduction in cinemas is now so good that it is sometimes possible to see and hear a film without being aware of the fact that loudspeakers are in use. Examples of current cinema practice may, therefore, be of interest.

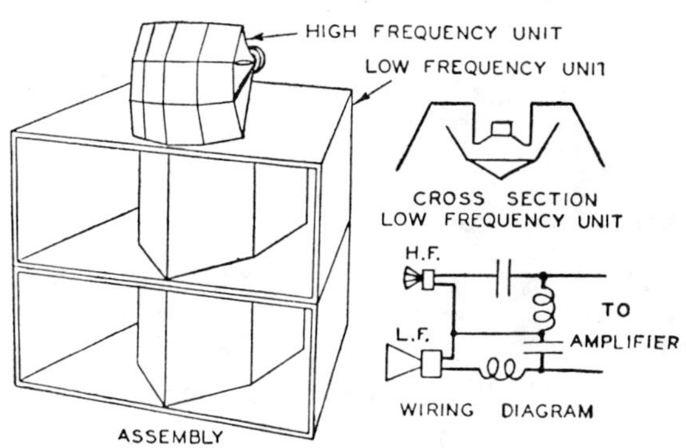


FIG. 26.—A two-channel theatre loudspeaker system consisting of a folded low frequency horn unit and a multicellular horn high frequency unit.

*From Olson's Elements of Acoustical Engineering—*

> "This loudspeaker consists of a low frequency folded horn unit for reproduction from 40 to 300 cycles and a multicellular horn unit for reproduction from 300 to 8,000 cycles. In order to minimize time delay and phase distortion due to a large path length difference between the low and high frequency horns, the effective length of the horns must be practically the same. The difference in path length is made relatively small by employing a short folded horn for bass, coupled to a large diameter speaker unit.
>
> The high frequency horn consists of a cluster of relatively small horns coupled to a common throat. The throat is coupled to one or more speaker units depending upon the power requirements . The dividing network introduces phase shift as well as a loss in power of 2 or more db."

---

Many cinema installations now employ bass reflex cabinets in place of folded horns.

FIG. 27.—R.C.A. Cinema Unit for theatres seating 1,500 upwards. Total height 10 feet. Total weight $\frac{1}{4}$ ton.

*Photo by courtesy of R.C.A. Photophone, Ltd.*

The low frequency unit consists of a folded horn to which two 15-inch speakers are coupled. The high frequency unit is a multi-cellular horn coupled to two high frequency loudspeaker units, mounted in such a way that it can be "angled" properly. A dividing network with a cross-over frequency of about 400 cycles is usually adopted.

For smaller theatres, a similar system, using one speaker for low and one for high frequencies is used, with a power handling capacity of 20 or more watts.

It will be noted that in all these cinema systems the high frequency source is placed immediately above the low frequency unit, and the latter covers a large area. The best position behind the screen is always chosen for the installation.

CHAPTER XVI

# ROOM ACOUSTICS

Most people realise that the listening room has a good deal of effect on the reproduction of speech and music. The size and shape and furnishings all play their part. Carpets and curtains absorb the higher frequencies. A set or speaker which sounds bright and clear in the shop may sound muffled and resonant at home, and it is advisable to select a bright tone when choosing in a showroom with little or no soft furnishings about, where the reverberation period may well be twice as long as in a furnished room.

Placing a loudspeaker in the corner of a room improves the radiation impedance seen by the cone, and also increases the low note radiation by use of the walls and floor as reflecting planes. In fact, a corner is so obviously the best position that it is surprising it is so rarely utilised. Fig. 28 shows the various equivalent reflecting planes and their effect. One speaker at B radiates as much low frequency energy as two at location A, and one at E equals two at D, or four at C.

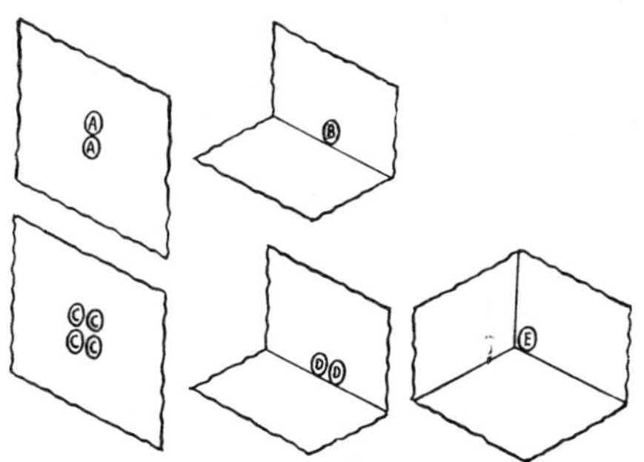


FIG. 28.
*From Henney's Radio Engineering Handbook*

It will be understood that merely placing a speaker in a corner will not have the full effect of actually mounting the speaker in a wall, as shown at positions B. D and E.

This question of radiation impedance accounts for the fact that even a little speaker sounds better in a large room than in a small one. It also explains why a larger room does not require an increase of power in proportion to the increase of size. The loudspeaker supplies maximum energy to the room when the room impedance is high, or when the speaker is near a pressure maximum ([1]). No resonance pressure maximum occurs at the speaker below the lowest resonant frequency of the room, and good low note response is therefore hard to obtain in small rooms.

(1) *Radio Engineering Handbook, p.* **921.**

The reproduction of a pure tone requires a room at least half as long as the wavelength of the note. Thus bottom C at 32 cycles (wavelength 35 ft.) would require 17½ ft. minimum. It is also noticed that the fundamental speaker resonance is less marked when highly damped by looking into a high acoustical impedance; in other words, bass resonance is more pronounced in a small room than a large one, or when the speaker is wrongly placed in any medium-sized room. Corner positions also permit improved high note response because of the smaller solid angle the radiation has to cover, say 90 degrees instead of 180 degrees. It is also obvious that when a corner or end position is used, everybody in the room is normally in front of the speaker.

Acoustically the best position for a loudspeaker is mounted in a wall, looking into the longest length of the room, preferably from one corner. Although structural and domestic considerations generally rule it out, the arrangement is worth consideration, and various methods of mounting are illustrated in Fig. 29, with details of results actually experienced. (It is much easier to read about these tests than to make them !)

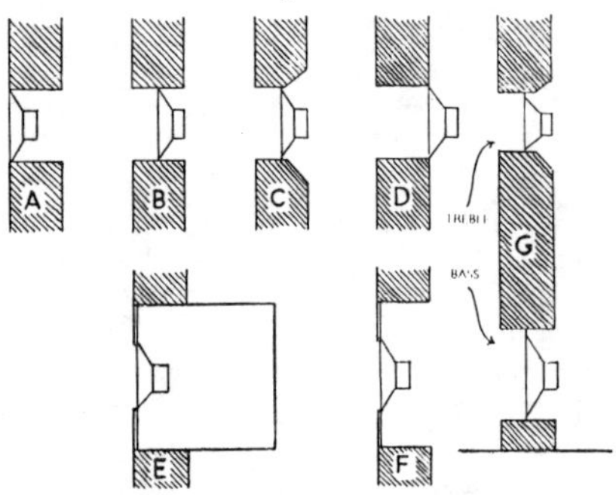


FIG. 29.—Various ways of mounting loud speakers in a party wall, with lounge in front and dining-room behind.

Results of actual tests made with a view to reproduction in two rooms (E excepted). In every case, high note radiation in front of the loudspeaker is better than behind, where the magnet acts as an obstruction to H. F.

*a.* Unsatisfactory because air pocket is formed at the back of the speaker. This method could be used with a wall not more than about 3″ thick.

*b.* Good results in front, poor H.F. at back.

*c.* Satisfactory both sides.

*d.* Unsatisfactory because air pocket is formed in front of the speaker.

*e.* Unit placed in box—not recommended—wall baffle largely wasted.

*f.* Sub-baffle should be very small and heavy, otherwise benefits of wall are dissipated.

*g.* Two speakers with cross-over. Bass unit near floor for improved L. F. radiation. H.F. unit about 3 ft. higher (say 4 ft. from floor) for natural effect in speech and solos.

It is difficult to arrange a speaker for best results on speech and music, as the former requires a single source effect, but music

*Absorption Coefficients of Various Materials*

| Material. | Frequencies in cycles/sec. | | |
|---|---|---|---|
| | 250. | 500. | 1,000–2,000. |
| Ordinary wall and ceiling surfaces: | | | |
| Lime plaster | 0·02–0·03 | 0·03–0·04 | 0·03 |
| Hard plaster | 0·01–0·02 | 0·01–0·02 | 0·02–0·03 |
| Unpainted brick | 0·03 | 0·03 | 0·05 |
| Wood-panelling, 3-ply | 0·01–0·02 | 0·01–0·02 | 0·01–0·02 |
| Curtains: | | | |
| Cretonne | — | 0·15 | — |
| Medium weight | — | 0·2–0·4 | — |
| Heavy, in folds | — | 0·5–1·0 | — |
| Floor coverings: | | | |
| Wood block in mastic | 0·03 | 0·06 | 0·10 |
| Cork carpet, ¼ in. thick | 0·03 | 0·07 | 0·20 |
| Porous rubber sheet, ¼ in. thick | 0·05 | 0·05 | 0·20 |
| Axminster carpet, ¼ in. thick | 0·05 | 0·10 | 0·35 |
| ,, ,, on ¼-in. felt underlay | 0·05 | 0·40 | 0·65 |
| ,, ,, on ¼-in. rubber ,, | 0·05 | 0·20 | 0·45 |
| Turkey carpet, ½ in. thick | 0·10 | 0·25 | 0·30 |
| ,, ,, on ½-in. felt underlay | 0·30 | 0·50 | 0·65 |
| Special absorbents: | | | |
| Acoustic plasters (½ to 1 in. thick) on stone | 0·15 | 0·25 | 0·30 |
| Fibre boards, plain, ½ in. thick, on battens | 0·30–0·40 | 0·30–0·35 | 0·25–0·35 |
| Medium efficiency tiles, on battens | 0·40 | 0·40 | 0·50 |
| High-efficiency tiles, with perforated surfaces, on battens | 0·50 | 0·80 | 0·85 |
| Acoustic felts, 1 in. thick, perforated covers on hard surface | 0·30 | 0·70 | 0·80 |
| Acoustic felts, ½ in. thick, on battens | 0·25 | 0·45 | 0·70 |
| Wood wool-cement board, 1 in. thick, on battens | 0·30 | 0·60 | 0·70 |
| Sprayed asbestos. 1 in. thick | 0·50–0·60 | 0·65–0·75 | 0·60–0·75 |
| Slag wool or glass silk about 2 in. thick, on battens | 0·70 | 0·85 | 0·90 |
| Cabot quilt, 3-ply, two layers | 0·40 | 0·70 | 0·70 |
| Individual objects in open-window units (ft.): | | | |
| Audience per person | 4·3 | 4·7 | 5·0 |
| Chairs, bent ash | 0·16 | 0·17 | 0·21 |
| Cushions, hair, 2¾ sq. ft. under canvas and plush | 1·1 | 1·8 | 1·5 |

FIG. 30. ***From Wood's Physics of Music***

should come from a wider source, especially in the bass. Practically all instruments with good low note output have a wide diffusion—the organ, piano, double bass, drums, etc. — and however good the loudspeaker it is never quite natural to hear a 75 piece orchestra bursting out of a 10″ or 12″ circle.

It is therefore suggested that the best compromise is to have two units, preferably in a corner position, with the bass well diffused near the floor, and the treble speaker immediately above. If only one speaker is used, some form of reflex or acoustic loading (see Chapter XIII) is a distinct help in diffusion effects.

The reverberation period of a room depends upon its size and the absorption coefficients of its walls and contents. The Fig. 30 list may be of interest for comparing different materials and rooms, and will be useful to those considering the construction of special cabinets.

As the absorption of sound at high frequencies in passing through air is much greater than at low frequencies, a large room or hall requires stronger "top" response than a small room for natural results. If you find that some forms of reproduction are too bright or shrill in a small room it is worth while to try the effect of an acoustic filter, by draping a piece of cloth across the front of the offending speaker. If material with an open weave be used, the H.F. attenuation will be small, but it can be intensified by using two or more layers. This form of high frequency control is often more subtle than the usual tone control.

CHAPTER XVII

# TRANSIENTS

There is a good deal of difference in loudspeakers in what is generally known as transient response. I want to use the term in its widest sense, to embrace attack as well as decay of sound. High flux density and stiff connection between speech coil and cone give good top note response and improved transients. Solid cabinets or baffles are also essential. Hard materials such as fired clay, and heavy steel or asbestos sheets which have a naturally high pitch or period are very good, and often improve transient response in comparison with wood.

The output impedance of the amplifier also affects the transient response of a loudspeaker. Fig. 31 shows at A the effect of a very high impedance such as Pentode or class "B" operation, at B a generator corresponding to class "A" operation, and at C very low impedance corresponding to negative feed back.

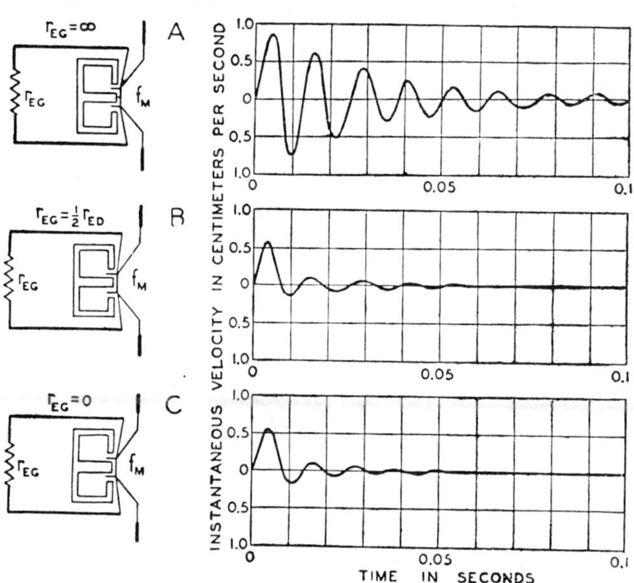


FIG. 31.—The transient response of a 12-inch loudspeaker to a unit force.
A. Generator of very high resistance.
B. Generator having a resistance of half the loudspeaker impedance.
C. Generator of zero impedance.

*From Olson's Elements of Acoustical Engineering*

The cone material and surround affect the transient response probably more than any other item. Hard, loud cones with apparent high note efficiency due to resonances, have very bad transient response. On the other hand, felted or linen cones with smoother response curve and lower acoustic output have much superior transient characteristics. In the same way, soft surrounds improve the transient response by adding dissipation to the edge of the cone with reduced reflection of the flexural wave. It is, of course, fairly obvious that as the cone is expected to respond to the vibrations which are forced upon it, any inherent resonances in the cone are undesirable and are bound to upset the transient position by reverberation. This phenomenon has been thoroughly investigated by the Research Dept. of the B.B.C. and a short description of the method is given under Distortion in Chapter I. It is confirmed that a speaker with peaky decay characteristics is untidy in a normal listening test.

If you take three identical driving systems of any size and fit (A) loud cone with corrugated surround ; (B) quiet non-resonant cone with corrugated surround ; (C) quiet cone with soft surround, you will find that switching from A to B and from B to C progressively reduces volume and improves quality. This happens every time with any size of speaker from $3\frac{1}{2}''$ up to $15''$ and simply confirms

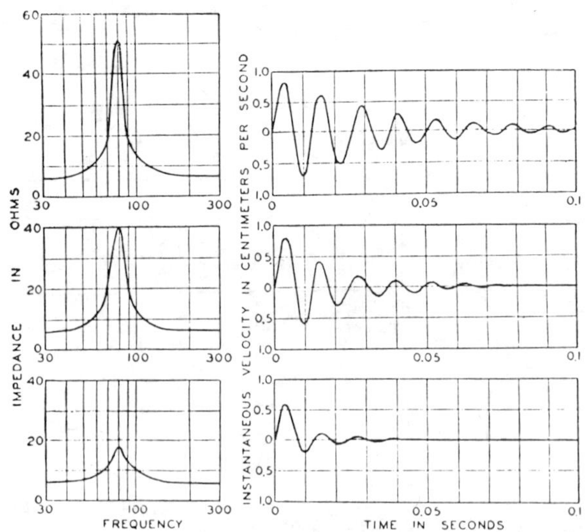


FIG. 32.—The unit force response of a loudspeaker coupled to a generator of very high resistance for different values of internal mechanical resistance—indicated by impedance curve.

*From Olson's Elements of Acoustical Engineering*

expectations. If you now take three of the small units and use them as microphones you will find similar improvements in quality but even more pronounced. Incidentally, the best speaker tests for these transient qualities are speech and full orchestra.

The effect of the bass resonance on transient response is clearly shown in Fig. 32.

It will be seen that a reduction of bass resonance or increase of mechanical resistance, as exemplified in a flatter impedance curve, improves the transient or decay element. It follows that improvements such as lowering the resonance frequency, or improving the air-loading by reflex or other methods, also help the transient position. With small cabinets or baffles the response to transients is usually very poor because the internal mechanical resistance is not sufficiently large.

The following diagram shows the transient effect of a narrow pulse (1 milli-second) at 50 pulses per second, in various loudspeakers. It will be seen that the pulse suffered slight distortion in passing through the amplifier. It is interesting to note that the following factors help to improve the transient response:—

1. High flux density.
2. Cloth surround to the cone, which reduces reflected resonance.
3. Absence of mechanical compliance in cone and coil assembly.
4. Heavy cone, which always reduces distortion when compared with a light cone.

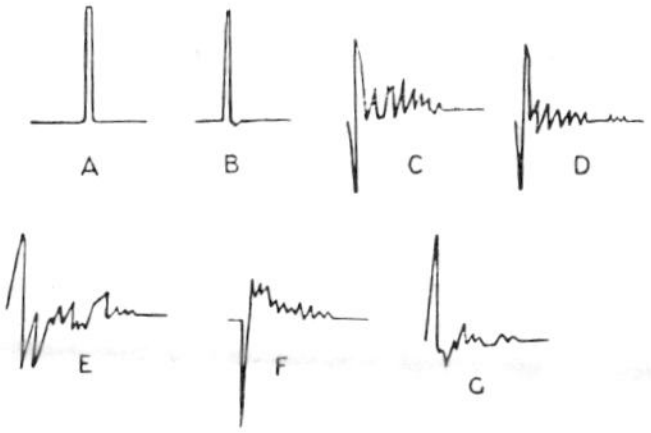

A B C D E F G

Fig. 32/1.

Pulse effect to show transient response of various loudspeakers

*a.* Input pulse to amplifier.
*b.* Output pulse from amplifier.
*c.* Output from 8″ speaker 8,000 lines, corrugated cone.
*d.* Output from 8″ speaker 13,000 lines, cloth surround.
*e.* Output from 10″ speaker 11,000 lines, with jointed cone.
*f.* Output from 10″ speaker 14,000 lines, heavy cone with cloth surround.
*g.* Output from 15″ speaker, 13,500 lines, heavy cone with cloth surround.

CHAPTER XVIII

# CROSSOVER NETWORKS

(Revised).

In order to extend the frequency range, and avoid intermodulation distortion between bass and treble, two loudspeakers may be used with a dividing network. The arrangement also facilitates the correct location of the speakers in the room, with the desirable combination of direction and diffusion. The obvious and simple plan of placing the treble unit immediately above the low note radiator as done in cinema installations is hard to beat. It is also possible to enjoy the full and distortionless bass of an acoustic chamber by adding an extra speaker in open back cabinet for high note radiation. Although the extra speaker may improve results if simply connected in parallel, the use of a separator or dividing network gives two important advantages : (*a*) full bass output is retained and (*b*) by keeping the low notes out of the top speaker, distortion due to the size of cabinet, cone resonance and intermodulation is eliminated.

For domestic use, a crossover at 1,000 cycles is satisfactory. It is difficult to improve on the following two circuits for efficiency and economy. FIG. 33A shows a half section parallel constant resistance filter giving attenuation at 12db. per octave with an insertion loss of about 2 db. FIG. 33B shows a quarter section series network, giving 6 to 8 db. attenuation per octave with an insertion loss of about 1 db. So far as quality of reproduction is concerned, there is little to choose between them. Component values for speakers of 3, 7½ and 15 ohms impedance are given.

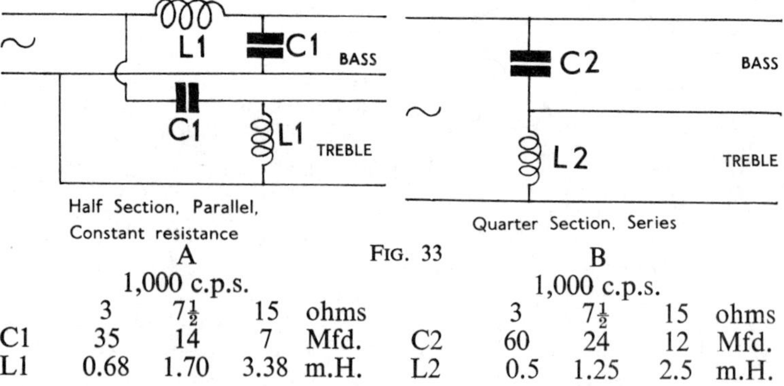


Half Section, Parallel, Constant resistance
A

Quarter Section, Series
B

FIG. 33

| A: 1,000 c.p.s. | 3 | 7½ | 15 | ohms |
|---|---|---|---|---|
| C1 | 35 | 14 | 7 | Mfd. |
| L1 | 0.68 | 1.70 | 3.38 | m.H. |

| B: 1,000 c.p.s. | 3 | 7½ | 15 | ohms |
|---|---|---|---|---|
| C2 | 60 | 24 | 12 | Mfd. |
| L2 | 0.5 | 1.25 | 2.5 | m.H. |

Considerable latitude in circuit values is permissible, as a perfect crossover at a fixed frequency is not required. Variations of 20 per cent. with circuit A or 30 per cent. with circuit B would offend the technical purist more than the musical ear. Speakers would normally be connected to the crossover network in phase, but the fact that deliberate out-of-phase connection often gives excellent results proves that a good deal of latitude may be enjoyed.

When circuit values are reasonably accurate, the impedance of two speakers remains about the same as a single speaker, as shown in the following diagram.

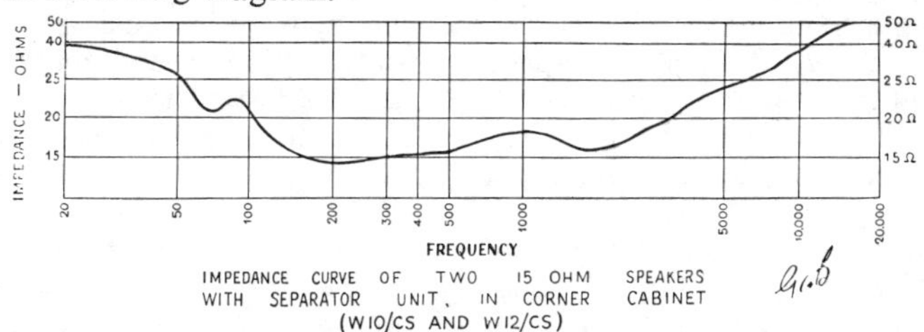


FIG. 34.—The improvement in performance resulting from this type of network is partly due to the improved level of impedance.

It is usual to use two speakers of similar impedance, but H.F. performance may be improved by adopting a lower impedance in the treble unit, thus overcoming the steep rise of impedance with frequency which has afflicted the moving coil speaker since birth. (I am told that a change of impedance on these lines may lead to instability with some amplifiers with heavy feedback circuit. I suggest that any amplifier which will not stand such small liberties with its output should be re-designed or be put in a glass case).

It is important that the two loudspeakers should be of equal sensitivity. A real difference in flux density results in a loss of naturalness and balance due mainly to difference in attack and transient response.

The L.F. unit may with advantage be larger than the H.F. speaker. A combination of 15″ bass and 8″ treble units is satisfactory provided the above remarks on flux density are borne in mind.

Resistance type volume controls tend to upset the response of crossover systems. Similar effects occur if an extra loudspeaker is connected in parallel with the input to the separator.

Tapped chokes or auto-transformers make satisfactory volume controls, provided the amplifier presents a low impedance source.

Air cored coils are generally advocated, but iron cores provide low resistance windings which may be worth while in cases where insertion loss must be kept as low as possible. Electrolytic condensers should not be used.

As regards crossover frequency, the component values are in inverse proportion to the frequency. Therefore, to cross over at 500 cycles instead of 1000 multiply all C & L values by 2. To cross over at 2,000 cycles instead of 1,000, divide all C & L values by 2.

## CHAPTER XIX

# NEGATIVE FEEDBACK

Most high quality amplifiers are now fitted with a certain amount of negative feedback in order to even out the response and reduce harmonic distortion. The system is most necessary where high impedance output valves such as pentodes and tetrodes are employed, as it reduces the output impedance and simplifies the problem of matching, as well as improving the transient response of the loudspeaker (see Chapter XVII). There is also a reduction in loudspeaker resonance, as shown in chapter XVII, Fig. 31/2.

There is always a danger of instability in an amplifier with negative feedback if the leakage inductance of the output transformer is not very low. The use of two speakers with a crossover network could expose such instability but would not cause it. If the amplifier is correctly designed and assembled, with a suitable output transformer, there is no danger of instability with a two- or three-speaker system and crossover network. In some cases, reversing the loudspeaker leads will effect a cure.

A striking example of the benefit of negative feedback in overcoming problems of load matching is to be seen in the high quality school equipment specially designed for Essex Education Committee. The 15 watt amplifier is coupled to a line transformer of low leakage inductance, which feeds the speaker lines at 300 ohms. Each of the 8 loudspeakers is fitted with a transformer so that the line load is matched when five speakers are in use. No provision is made for adjusting the transformer ratios when the number of speakers in use is varied. When only one speaker is in use the load is 1,500 ohms instead of 300 ohms, but the provision of negative feedback obliterates any trace of distortion from mis-matching.

## CHAPTER XX

# TRANSFORMERS AND MATCHING

The purpose of the Output Transformer is to match the low impedance of the loudspeaker to the high impedance of the output valve(s). An extra winding is often included for negative feedback, so that voltage is deliberately returned to the input stage out of phase with the incoming signals and so cancels out much of the distortion introduced in the equipment.

A glance at any typical impedance curve will show that the impedance of the loudspeaker varies at different frequencies, so that perfect matching is not possible. It is usual to work on the middle frequency range and accept the impedance at 400, 600, 800 or 1,000 cycles, according to taste. The impedance is always higher than the D.C. resistance of the speech coil, and it is satisfactory to assume a difference of 30% or 50%.

The higher the output impedance, the more important the matching becomes. Thus pentodes and tetrodes are more critical than triodes. Even so, quite wide variations may occur. When an extension speaker is connected to a set, this is what happens, according to Mr. Beaumont (our technical sub-editor) "The valve load may be almost halved, and the resulting mis-match may give an increase in power output (within limits) at the expense of harmonic distortion in the case of tetrode or pentode valves without feedback."

With the usual small extension speaker, results are satisfactory, but if a wide-range speaker is used any distortion is noticeable. If the output valve load is 7,000 ohms and the speakers are 3 ohms each, halving the load is equivalent to altering the transformer ratio from 48/1 to about 35/1.

Negative feedback reduces the output impedance and is doubly useful where an extension speaker is used, since it reduces the resulting rise in distortion. In fact, with really low impedance sources the question of matching becomes of secondary importance, and one 7½ ohm secondary can be used for 3 ohm or 15 ohm speakers. In fact, if the transformer winding is tapped for 3 ohm load, the quality of reproduction may be improved by using a 3 ohm speaker on the full 7½ ohm winding where the leakage inductance would be lower. The foregoing should not be construed to mean that load matching does not matter. Obviously, the most suitable transformer ratio will be adopted, with flexibility according to circumstances.

## RATIO-IMPEDANCE TABLE

| Transformer Ratio | Ratio Squared | SPEECH-COIL IMPEDANCE — OHMS | | | | | | | | Transformer Ratio |
|---|---|---|---|---|---|---|---|---|---|---|
| | | 2 | 3 | 4 | 6 | 8 | 10 | 12 | 15 | |
| 10/1 | 100 | 200 | 300 | 400 | 600 | 800 | 1,000 | 1,200 | 1,500 | 10/1 |
| 15/1 | 225 | 450 | 675 | 900 | 1,350 | 1,800 | 2,250 | 2,700 | 3,400 | 15/1 |
| 18/1 | 324 | 650 | 970 | 1,300 | 1,950 | 2,600 | 3,250 | 3,900 | 4,800 | 18/1 |
| 20/1 | 400 | 800 | 1,200 | 1,600 | 2,400 | 3,200 | 4,000 | 4,800 | 6,000 | 20/1 |
| 22/1 | 484 | 970 | 1,450 | 1,950 | 2,900 | 3 900 | 4,800 | 5,800 | 7,250 | 22/1 |
| 25/1 | 625 | 1,250 | 1,875 | 2,500 | 3,750 | 5,000 | 6,250 | 7,500 | 9,400 | 25/1 |
| 28/1 | 784 | 1,570 | 2,350 | 3,140 | 4,700 | 6,280 | 7,850 | 9,400 | 11,800 | 28/1 |
| 30/1 | 900 | 1,800 | 2,700 | 3,600 | 5,400 | 7,200 | 9,000 | 10,800 | 13,500 | 30/1 |
| 32/1 | 1,024 | 2,050 | 3,070 | 4,100 | 6,150 | 8,200 | 10,250 | 12,300 | 15,400 | 32/1 |
| 35/1 | 1,225 | 2,450 | 3,675 | 4,900 | 7,350 | 9,800 | 12,250 | 14,700 | 18,400 | 35/1 |
| 38/1 | 1,444 | 2,900 | 4,330 | 5,800 | 8,675 | 11,600 | 14,450 | 17,350 | 21,600 | 38/1 |
| 40/1 | 1,600 | 3,200 | 4,800 | 6,400 | 9,600 | 12,800 | 16,000 | 19,200 | 24,000 | 40/1 |
| 42/1 | 1,764 | 3,530 | 5,300 | 7,000 | 10,600 | 14,000 | 17,600 | 21,200 | 26,500 | 42/1 |
| 45/1 | 2,025 | 4,050 | 6,100 | 8,100 | 12,200 | 16,200 | 20,250 | 24,400 | 30,400 | 45/1 |
| 48/1 | 2,304 | 4,600 | 6,900 | 9,200 | 13,800 | 18,400 | 23,000 | 27,600 | ★ | 48/1 |
| 50/1 | 2,500 | 5,000 | 7,500 | 10,000 | 15,000 | 20,000 | 25,000 | 30,000 | ★ | 50/1 |
| 52/1 | 2,704 | 5,400 | 8,100 | 10,800 | 16,200 | 21,600 | 27,000 | 32,400 | ★ | 52/1 |
| 55/1 | 3,025 | 6,050 | 9,075 | 12,000 | 18,150 | 24,000 | 30,200 | ★ | ★ | 55/1 |
| 58/1 | 3,364 | 6,730 | 10,000 | 13,500 | 20,000 | 27,000 | 33,600 | ★ | ★ | 58/1 |
| 60/1 | 3,600 | 7,200 | 10,800 | 14,400 | 21,600 | 28,800 | ★ | ★ | ★ | 60/1 |
| 62/1 | 3,844 | 7,700 | 11,500 | 15,400 | 23,000 | 30,800 | ★ | ★ | ★ | 62/1 |
| 65/1 | 4,225 | 8,450 | 12,700 | 17,000 | 25,400 | 34,000 | ★ | ★ | ★ | 65/1 |
| 68/1 | 4,624 | 9,250 | 13,900 | 18,500 | 27,800 | ★ | ★ | ★ | ★ | 68/1 |
| 70/1 | 4,900 | 9,800 | 14,700 | 19,600 | 29,400 | ★ | ★ | ★ | ★ | 70/1 |
| 75/1 | 5,625 | 11,250 | 16,900 | 22,500 | 33,800 | ★ | | | | |
| 80/1 | 6,400 | 12,800 | 19,200 | 25,600 | ★ | ★ | | | | |
| 85/1 | 7,225 | 14,500 | 21,700 | 29,000 | ★ | ★ | | | | |
| 90/1 | 8.100 | 16,200 | 24,300 | 32,400 | ★ | ★ | | | | |
| 95/1 | 9,025 | 18,000 | 27,000 | ★ | ★ | ★ | | | | |
| 100/1 | 10,000 | 20,000 | 30,000 | ★ | ★ | ★ | | | | |

*N.B Half any Ratio = Quarter Impedance Double Ratio = 4 times Impedance.*
*Speech-coil Impedance at 800 cycles is generally about 30% higher than its D.C Resistance*

FIG. 35.

The frequency response of transformers is usually so much better than loudspeakers that response curves are rarely considered necessary. The L.F. response depends on the inductance being high enough to suit the valve and the H.F. response depends on low leakage inductance, apart from turns ratio. The power and current capacity depends on the size of the core and thickness of wire.

When a transformer is centre-tapped there is a difference in the resistance of the two halves of the winding due to increasing size as the coil is wound, unless the windings are placed side by side, or are wound in four or more sections and balanced out. These differences in D.C. resistance are of no account for ordinary requirements.

Where the highest possible quality is required, with level response up to 15,000 cycles or more, it is customary to wind the primary and secondary in 8 or more alternating sections, thus achieving the tightest possible coupling and reducing leakage inductance to a minimum. The primary sections are then connected in such a way that equal resistance is obtained in each half. Such transformers take a long time to make and are naturally expensive.

The inductance of a transformer primary is largely controlled by the number of turns and the quality of the laminations.

The following are suggested as a rough indication of requirements for good quality—

| | | |
|---|---|---|
| Minimum Inductance—Power Triode | —20 Henrys | |
| ,, ,, —Pentode | —50 ,, | |
| Maximum Leakage Inductance | — 0.1 Henry | |
| Minimum Core Size for 5 Watts—approx. | ¾″ × 2″ | |
| ,, ,, ,, ,, 10 ,, | ,, | 1″ × 3″ |
| ,, ,, ,, ,, 15 ,, | ,, | 1¼″ × 4″ |

## CHAPTER XXI

# COMPARING PERFORMANCE

This is by no means so simple as it sounds. Anybody can hear the difference between a very poor speaker and a very good one, but when we have to compare two better-quality speakers there are many pitfalls.

It is necessary to bear in mind that the reproduction depends on the quality of the input, and if this quality is bad or distorted a better speaker will expose the distortion and sound worse than an inferior one. The B.B.C. are by no means blameless in this respect.

B.B.C. quality when it is good, is very, very good, but some transmissions are very bad and any attempt to judge speaker performance on a bad transmission will give misleading results. The same reservations apply to pick-ups, records and amplifiers. Many amplifiers suffer from H.F. distortion or oscillation which only shows up on a speaker with appreciable response above 10,000 cycles. Most pick-ups require bass lift and some require top cut on commercial recordings.

Take another case. Assume that your equipment cuts off a 5,000 cycles and you have one speaker with a smooth response up to 10,000 and another with peaks at 4,000/5,000 and nothing above 7,000 cycles. The latter would sound better. Still another case : Assume your equipment falls off badly in the bass below 100 cycles, and you have one speaker with bass resonance at 70/80 cycles and another with resonance at 30/40 cycles. The former would appear to have the better bass response.

However, let us assume that the available quality is good, and the loudspeakers are equally matched to the output impedance. If you mean business you will arrange a switch so that immediate comparisons can be made in the same passage of music. It is no use waiting until somebody changes the wires, as the ear forgets tonal quality or timbre very quickly. The quickest test is on full orchestral or dance music. Listen carefully to the bass and try to differentiate between a true note and resonance. The triangle, cymbals and snare drums are good for extreme top. Do not mistake cone resonance around 3,000/5000 cycles for top response. Drums and hand-clapping are excellent for comparing frequency response because difference-tones and harmonics do not arise to deceive the ear.

Needle scratch is also a useful source of sound, which covers a much wider frequency range than any musical instrument. Notice the general drop in pitch of about an octave when the needle is on the centre groove compared with the outside groove of a record.

The oboe has the highest overtones, and the organ goes down the lowest. The piano is not a searching test as it comes out well even with considerable top and bass cut. (See Fig. 10,Chapter IX). The violin is a good test for smoothness in the upper middle register, where peaks give a tinny effect to the tone.

Listen for clarity and transient response on full orchestral passages. A speaker which sorts out the instruments will not have any difficulty in dealing with solos. Try to distinguish true sensitivity from mere loudness. Flux density is expensive. It improves attack and adds life to the reproduction, whereas resonances increase the volume only at certain frequencies and blur the results. Allow for difference in position. If one unit is mounted near the floor, remember that high notes are directional and will only reach your ears by reflection.

Speech is an essential test, and most people judge its reproduction accurately. The first test imposed on a loudspeaker by the Research Department of the B.B.C. is to listen to the reproduction of speech in the middle of a field, away from reflecting surfaces, and compare it with the original voice. A good loudspeaker should give good reproduction of speech, but it does not of necessity follow that it will be equally good on music, which requires a much wider frequency range.

As regards ability to judge quality of reproduction, this depends on the gift of tonal discrimination, which is not the same as musical talent. A musician must be gifted in the sense of musical pitch, intensity and rhythm, but he may be no better than the average in appreciation of actual tone quality.

Although this capacity for tone judgment is more likely to be found in musical people than in others, it is possible for an unmusical person to be strongly gifted in this direction—with an ear for tone and no ear for tune.

CHAPTER XXII.

# LOUDSPEAKER LIFE

The question "How long will it last ?" is often asked about a loudspeaker, but so much depends upon the conditions of use that it is impossible to give a plain answer. A loudspeaker in a steam laundry may wilt in a few weeks, whereas the same type may last 10 or 15 years in a dry atmosphere. Tropical finishes will help a loudspeaker to resist extremes of climatic conditions, but reasonable protection from exposure is obviously necessary. Damp, dirt and metal filings are the loudspeaker's greatest enemies.

Given reasonable conditions, the best way to estimate length of service is by actual experience. I know of two or three extension speakers which have been in regular use for more than 14 years. The cabinets have been well cared for and are almost as new, and the performance is still satisfactory.

I have come to the conclusion that cones improve with age, especially under dry conditions. It is also clear that the continual movement of the cone assembly during use tends to free the suspension and lower the bass resonance. These factors often result in an improvement in quality as time goes on. I will cite two personal experiences in support of this rather interesting point. My friend, Mr. Beaumont, of Ambassador Radio, recently devoted many hours to the calculation of the correct exponential reflex corner loading for a 12 inch speaker for which we supplied a specially made unit with soft suspension. I was surprised to be told by Mr. Beaumont that the new speaker was not so good as an old one which had been used for the development tests. An examination with oscillator revealed the fact that the old speaker, which had a bass resonance at 65 cycles some five years ago, was now down to 35 cycles on open baffle, having absorbed a good deal of punishment during the period. As the resonance of the new unit was about 45 cycles, and as these technical men are hard to please, we had perforce to build another speaker with more compliance in the centring device.

My second illustration comes from Holland—a small country of which I am rather fond, as it was the only one in the world to import our speakers before the war. When I re-visited the country early in 1947, I was shown two loudspeakers which were nearly ten years old and which had been carefully preserved during the German occupation. Originally 10,000 lines, I estimated that the flux density had dropped to 9,000. In the post-war model the flux density had been stepped up to over 12,000 lines, and my agents promised to make a comparison immediately new supplies were received. I was again surprised to be informed in due course that the quality of reproduction of the old speakers was preferred, in spite of the difference in sensitivity. It was found that the bass resonance had dropped from 70 cycles to nearly 50, and the maturity of the cones was having its usual effect. Such a test is only possible in the rather unusual case where a certain type of unit has been continued for a number of years.

I hope the reader will forgive the personal tone of this chapter, but it seems to be the easiest way to answer the original question. It means that, with careful use, the performance of a good loudspeaker can reasonably be expected to improve, just as the tone of a good piano settles down after the first year or two. One gathers from remarks made by Mr. Shorter of the B.B.C. Research Station during a recent lecture that they have loudspeakers of pre-war vintage, (I believe about 1934/5) of which they still think very highly.

## CORROSION

A peculiar (and fortunately uncommon) cause of Loudspeaker breakdown is corrosion of the voice coil wire. This may take the form of green-spot on the coil itself, or in severe cases the whole length of the copper wire from the coil to the eyelet in the cone may be covered by verdigris which eats into the copper and eventually causes an open circuit.

It is fairly certain that these effects are due to abnormal atmospheric conditions. Salt-laden air and proximity to chemical works appear to be prime causes. Coating the voice coil winding and leads with suitable varnish will usually protect the copper from this form of corrosion.

Where conditions conducive to corrosion are known to exist, it is advisable to protect the speaker unit by wrapping in cellophane or P.V.C. sheeting—even at the cost of some acoustic efficiency. In one installation in a chemical factory it was found necessary to run the extension wiring in lead-covered cable to overcome frequent breakdown.

## CHAPTER XXIII

# DOPPLER EFFECT

At least one writer has suggested that the treble note in a loudspeaker becomes frequency modulated by the bass note through the Doppler effect, but this hardly seems to matter at the velocity attained by the speech coil. Doppler's principle explains why the pitch of a locomotive whistle appears to drop sharply as the engine passes the observer. The speed of the engine is added to the velocity of the sound as it approaches and is deducted as it recedes. Thus, if the frequency of the whistle is 550, the wavelength is 2 ft. If the engine approaches at 60 m.p.h. or 88 ft./sec. the wavelength

becomes $\frac{1{,}100 - 88}{550} = 1.84$ ft, which is 598 cycles.

When the engine recedes the wavelength is

$$\frac{1{,}100 + 88}{550} = 2.16 \text{ ft} = 509 \text{ cycles.}$$

The difference is equal to a drop of two notes on the piano, D to B.

In the same way, the forward and backward movement of the moving-coil must have some effect on the frequency of other notes. Assume an exceptional movement of $\frac{1}{4}''$ each way at 50 cycles, and the speed is only about 2 ft. per second, which would cause a 550 cycle note to vary between 552 and 548. Such changes would rarely occur in actual use, and would not be noticeable at the rate of 50 per second. They should not be confused with vibrato, which involves a change of pitch of about half a tone at the rate of about 6 per second.

---

**DOPPLER EFFECT**

Further investigation reveals that the maximum velocity of the speech coil under the above conditions is 7 ft/sec. This is equivalent to variations of $\pm$3.2 cycles at 500 or $\pm$32 at 5,000 c.p.s. This is about one-tenth of a semitone and as piano tuning or the warming-up of an orchestra may vary one-tenth of a semi-tone, the change can be ignored in a loudspeaker.

## CHAPTER XXIV

# PHASE EFFECTS

The increasing use of negative feedback, acoustic loading and cross-over networks involves more serious consideration of phase effects.

As everybody knows, waves which are out of phase cancel out, and the need for baffles and cabinets arises to prevent the sound waves from the back of the speaker reaching the frontal waves out of phase. This only occurs where the wavelength is long enough.

The following diagram will make this clear. The curves A to E represent two full waves travelling in opposite directions, and the second line shows the position after they have travelled one quarter wavelength. They are completely cancelled out.

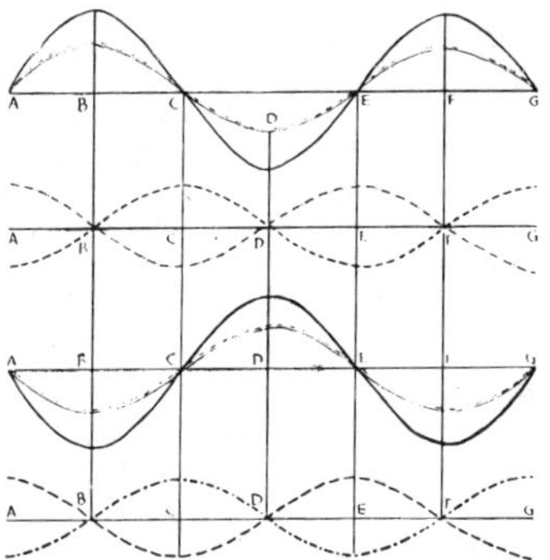


*From Wood's "Sound Waves and their Uses.* *(Blackie)*

FIG. 36.—Stationary waves due to two equal sets of waves travelling in opposite directions. The broken line with dots represents waves travelling to the left. The broken line without dots represents waves travelling to the right. Four successive instants are shown.

On the top line the two sets of waves are in phase, with the result shown by the continuous line. The second line shows the position after the direct and reflected waves have travelled one quarter of a wavelength. The two waves are now in exactly opposite phase. In the third line we see the position after the waves have moved through a further quarter of a wavelength, and the fourth line shows the waves again in opposition.

It will be seen from the foregoing that at a quarter wavelength the vibrations from each side of a loudspeaker will cancel out if they are allowed to meet. A 5 ft baffle with 2′ 6″ radius would therefore start to cut off at 110 cycles, because the wavelength of this note is 10 ft. (see Piano Chart, Chapter IX) and the quarter wavelength is 2′ 6″. With a square baffle, the distance increases at the corners, so that cut off is not sharply defined. A circular baffle with the speaker mounted in the middle would be a very poor system.

## TWO SPEAKERS

If two cabinet speakers are placed one on top of the other and connected in parallel and in phase, moving one of them back 12 inches will throw them out of phase at 256 cycles (Middle C) and the output at this frequency drops 9 db. (this is quarter wavelength). Similarly, if they are connected out of phase, the movement increases the output. On musical reproduction the difference is quite audible, and the middle register may be seriously affected by wrong placing of twin speakers, as even a few inches may be of importance.

It will be noted that a quarter wavelength is always the first antinode at position B in the curve.

## REFLECTION

When a sound wave strikes a flat surface it is reflected out of phase, and the curves shown in Fig. 36 are arrived at by reflecting a pure sound wave and finding the stationary points by exploring with a flame which is moved by the vibrations. The positions where the waves are cancelled are known as standing waves. When a loudspeaker is placed across the smallest diameter of a room, with a wall in front and behind, the standing waves are obviously increased by reflection from the two walls.The speaker should be placed facing the longest length, or better still, in one corner of the room, so that standing wave effect is reduced as much as possible, just as in a concert hall of oblong shape, the platform is always placed at one end.

## PHASE INVERSION

When we come to consider Reflex (or phase inversion) Cabinets and Acoustic Labyrinths, we immediately meet with a difficulty. It is claimed for the Reflex Cabinet that the phase of low notes is inverted, and they are brought out through the port in phase with the frontal waves from the cone to improve the bass, whereas the Acoustic Labyrinth is designed to emit through the opening out of phase at either fundamental or air-column resonance.

To phase or not to phase, that is the question.

In an effort to clarify the situation, a number of tests were made, using a noise level or phon meter in a room about 20 ft. square.

No claim to absolute accuracy is made, but it was found that, at different frequencies, diverting the port emission from the microphone had differing results, as follows—

*a.* Increase of volume by 2/4 db.
*b.* No change.
*c.* Decrease in volume by 2/8 db.

It was concluded that at (*a*) the port emission was out of phase with frontal waves from the speaker, gradually shifting through (*b*) to the same phase as speaker at (*c*). Condition (*c*) is, of course, the result of phase inversion in the cabinet. The following is a summary of the results—

## DETAILS OF TESTS FOR PHASING

| *Test No.* | *Unit* | *Cabinet* | *Size* | *Resonances Cycles* | *Out of Phase at Cycles* |
|---|---|---|---|---|---|
| 1 | 8″ | Reflex | 30″ × 15″ × 8″ | 45, 75, and 120 | 30, 90 and 120 |
| 2 | 10″ | Reflex | 30″ × 15″ × 12″ | 35, 60 and 95 | 65 |
| 3 | 8″ | Reflex | 30″ × 15″ × 15″ | 70 and 100 | 30 and 75 |
| 4 | 12″ | Reflex | 30″ × 16″ × 16″ without Reflector | 35 and 90 | none |
| 5 | 12″ | Reflex | 30″ × 16″ × 16″ with Reflector | 30 and 90 | 80 and 200 |
| 6 | 8″ | Acoustic Labyrinth | 30″ × 15″ × 12″ | 40, 90, 122 and 180 | 80 and 240 |

In all cases the fundamental cone resonance is the first.

TEST NO. 3—Cabinet in ½″ plaster-board not quite air tight.

TEST NO. 6.—Note extra resonances from increased reflecting surfaces.

It appears that the Reflex type of cabinet actually performs as a phase inverter over the major portion of the low frequency range, but phase shift is also affected by the resistance of the system.

The out-of-phase effects recorded by sensitive phon-meter were not noticeable by the ear. In Test No. 4 no out-of-phase emission could be traced and it is assumed that the cone took control. When a reflector was fitted in the cabinet to fold the air-column or pipe, fundamental resonance dropped from 35 to 30 cycles, the air-column resonance remained at 90, and out-of-phase readings from port were found at 80 and 200 cycles. Interior reflectors therefore seem to damp the cone and increase the wavelength, thus affecting phasing, without making much difference to the main air-column resonance which is the most important and noticeable element of all these systems of acoustic loading.

## ACOUSTIC LABYRINTH

Test No. 6 was made to check the phase readings. The transmission line in the cabinet was about 40 inches long. At a quarter wavelength this gives us 13′ 4″, which is 83 cycles. The test gave strong out-of-phase effects at 75/85 cycles which were distinctly audible, and which were in line with expectations. Although not quite matched to the cabinet, the bass output from the 8″ unit had rock-like steadiness and was considered superior to a similar Reflex cabinet, but there is some absorption of H.F. response by the felt lining. In view of the prominence of air-column resonance, it is suggested that the wavelength should be calculated to be out of phase at this frequency rather than at cone resonance. In any case, a cone resonance at 42 cycles would need a transmission line some 7 ft. long.

## FEEDBACK

In the case of negative feedback, volts from the output transformer are returned to the input valve out of phase. It follows, therefore, that when two speakers are used there is a possibility of trouble if the speakers are incorrectly phased. Reversing connections will usually put things right. There appears to be less danger of oscillation when a separate winding is used for the feedback circuit, as the speaker loading affects the phase relations in its driving winding to a larger extent than in a suitable tertiary winding.

## PARALLEL

It is well-known that two speakers in parallel, side by side, must be connected in phase. They should also be placed in the same frontal plane, as a difference of 12″ would throw them out of phase at about 256 cycles (middle C). Loudspeakers used at opposite ends of the room would be connected out of phase, although this arrangement is not recommended.

When a cross-over network is used, the same phase effects do not arise, and results are often improved by connecting the two speakers out of phase.

---

**Phasing.** To check the phasing of two loudspeakers, connect a torch battery to the speech coil and the cone will jump in or out of the gap ; mark positive and negative accordingly. The phase is due to the direction of the speech coil winding and the polarity of the magnet.

## CHAPTER XXV

# LOUDSPEAKER EFFICIENCY

There appears to be a good deal of doubt about the actual loss of power in the loudspeaker, in terms of watts output compared with watts input.

In one instance, it is stated that a 600 watt amplifier would be required to give symphony orchestra power of 30 watts from speakers on large baffles. This estimate is obviously based on 5% efficiency, but in view of the enormous volume available from even a 20 watt amplifier, the estimate appears to be wide of the mark. Many cinemas are run with 20 watt equipment and speaker systems similar to the R.C.A. illustration in Chapter XV are actually rated at 50% efficiency.

The latest calculations for the power radiated by a full orchestra give 70 watts at full volume, with 0.4 watts for the piano (see Chapter VIII). Taking the piano at 0.4 watts as a basis for comparison, the following tests were made for L.F. efficiency on four types of speaker, in a room of average size, care being taken to avoid resonance points where output is much greater.

| *Type of Speaker* | *Mounting* | *Flux Density* | *Input 50/200 cycles* | *Average Output* | *Average Efficiency* |
|---|---|---|---|---|---|
| 12″ Cloth Surround | Infinite Baffle | 13,000 | 1.1 watt | 0.12 watt | 11% |
| 12″ Corrugated | Reflex Cabinet | 13,000 | 1.1 ,, | 0.24 ,, | 22% |
| 8″ Corrugated | Small open-back Cabinet | 10,000 | 1.1 ,, | 0.06 ,, | 5½% |
| 8″ Corrugated | Reflex Cabinet | 10,000 | 1.1 ,, | 0.15 ,, | 16½% |

These figures are only intended as a rough guide.

The extra power at low frequency from Reflex loading is very noticeable.

---

These efficiency tests were only made at low frequencies because the readings at higher frequencies are seriously affected by standing waves and pressure points in ordinary rooms. As the room and walls are considered as part of the loudspeaker system the total efficiency is the interesting point. Estimates of dead room efficiency are of no interest to the average listener.

## REFLEX CABINETS SPECIAL NOTE

The question of phase inversion was studied in Chapter 13 chiefly with a view to obtaining best results in cabinets of normal domestic size. Another approach is to calculate the preferred size for a given type of speaker so that the acoustic reactance and radiation resistance of air chamber and aperture match the cone at resonance. This means that the air-column and cone resonances occur at the same frequency. I am indebted to Mr. D. L. Hillman of Coventry for some interesting calculations based on an article which appeared in "Electronics and S. W. World" in 1941. The following examples are given as a basis for experiment :-

| Unit | Piston dia. of cone | Open resonance | CHAMBER | | Cubic ft. | PORT AREA |
|---|---|---|---|---|---|---|
| A. 8″ | 6″ | 80 cycles | 32 x 16 x 12″ | = | 2.5 | 28 sq. ins. |
| B. 8″ | 6″ | 80 cycles | 31 x 16½ x 15½ | = | 3.5 | 44 sq. ins. |
| C. 10″ | 7½″ | 70 cycles | 38 x 18 x 15″ | = | 4.33 | 44 sq. ins. |
| D. 12″ | 9½″ | 60 cycles | 50 x 20 x 16″ | = | 7 | 70 sq. ins. |

Cabinet B has been tested. There is perfect phase inversion down to 40 cycles with no trace of frequency doubling at reasonable power. Examples A. C. and D are calculated and may need "tuning" by varying port area. Cabinets may also be "tuned" by inserting a pipe or tube of cone-piston diameter behind the port and varying its length.

The system offers definite advantages, especially to speakers of smaller size, but if an extra speaker is not used for top response, the resonance should be below 75 cycles to avoid colouration of speech.

An article by Mr. C. T. Chapman in the "Wireless World" of October 1949, entitled "Vented Loudspeaker Cabinets," gives an outline of the calculations required for this form of matching.

## CONCLUSION

There is a small supplement to this book giving commercial examples of some of the acoustic arrangements which have been considered. The selection has been quite haphazard and is not intended to be either representative or complete.

As regards the general question of reproduction, although there is a scientific explanation for all that happens, it is largely a question of opinion and taste. Many of the statements made are simply the writer's opinion. The human ear is very accommodating, but it still remains one of the most delicate and elaborate of instruments known to man, and it must be the final judge of all loudspeaker results. If this book has thrown some light on the subject, and if it has given some interesting details of the problems of loudspeaker design and performance, it has achieved its object.

# SUPPLEMENT

## AMBASSADOR

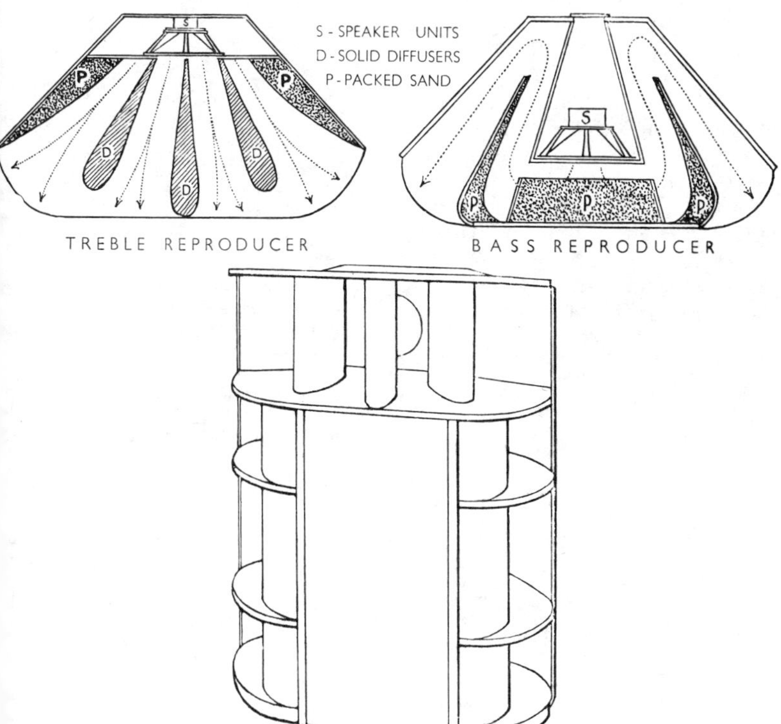


An interesting example of a folded exponential horn for bass, with four short virtual horns for treble.

The bass flare has a nominal cut-off at 65 cycles, but this is extended downwards by the walls of the room to an extent determined by the physical characteristics of the room itself. The pressure at the back of the cone is relieved by a small aperture at the apex of the inner chamber.

The cross-over network is carried out at high impedance and occurs at 375 c.p.s.

The complete unit handles an average input of 15 watts without break-up as a result of structural rigidity, all non-conductive cavities being packed with sand. A 12-inch unit for bass, and 8-inch with large magnet for treble, are fitted, both with cloth suspension. This speaker is installed and may be heard at the Weydale Hotel, North Bay, Scarborough.

SUPPLEMENT,

# VOIGT

As an example of the study of room acoustics, the Voigt Corner Horn was well ahead of its time. The efficiency range of the exponential horn was extended by reflectors for treble and a resonance chamber for bass, while full advantage was taken of the corner position. The natural effect of solo pieces leaving the loudspeaker at 3 to 5 ft. above floor level, with wide diffusion of low notes, was also achieved.

Very high flux density was a further feature of the system.

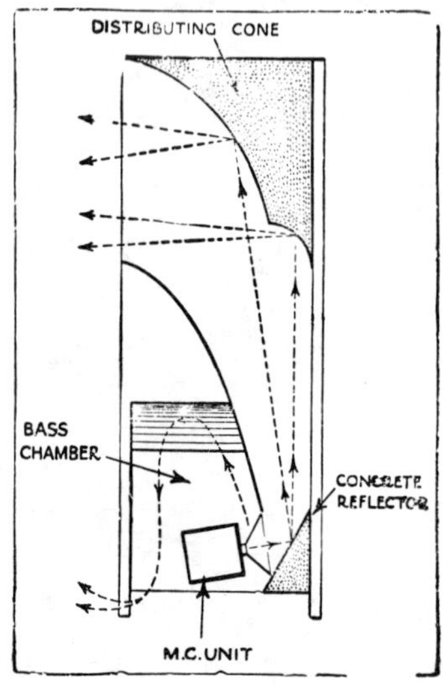


# BARKER

The Barker speaker is an interesting example of a dual drive system. An aluminium tube replaces the usual non-metallic coil former, with a thin layer of rubber, over which is wound a suitable coil. At low frequencies the coil provides the drive, but at high frequencies the coil inertia reduces movement and the aluminium former eventually takes charge and itself drives the cone. This change occurs progressively above 5,000 c.p.s.

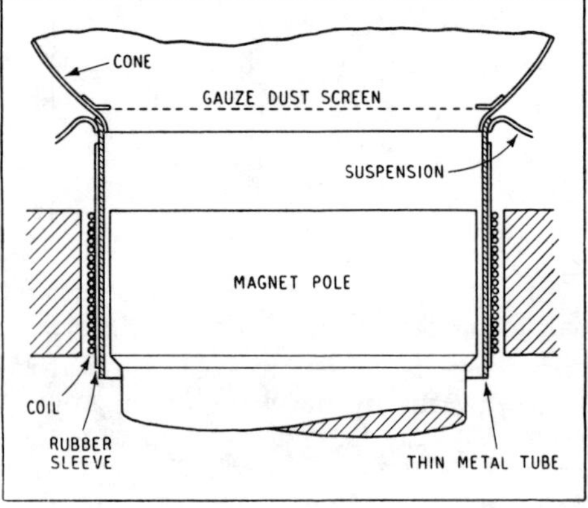


Construction of Barker Patent Dual Drive

The cone is formed from closely woven material impregnated with a synthetic resin and moulded under gentle heat.

The diameter of the speaker is $12\frac{1}{4}''$, and the peak input is 15 watts. Weight 13 lbs.

# WHARFEDALE
# SAND-FILLED PANEL

This arrangement gives results similar to the brick stucture described overleaf, with the advantages of easy installation and portability. Two plywood panels are spaced one inch apart, the space is filled with dry sand, and the complete assembly weighs about one hundredweight. A 15 inch cloth suspension unit is used for bass, producing a fundamental resonance below 30 c/s.

The treble speaker has open baffle mounting, and may be an 8″ or 10″ unit with crossover at 1000 c/s, or a high flux-density 5″ unit, as illustrated, with crossover at about 3000 c/s.

The height of the main structure is 40″, capacity 9 cu. ft. Peak input 15 watts. Standing wave effects inside the cavity may be reduced by placing two layers of felt, ¼″ thick, or one layer of ½″ felt, horizontally across the enclosure at a height of 18″ or 20″ from the floor, thus dividing the space into two compartments (B.B.C. patent).

# WHARFEDALE
# BRICK CORNER-REFLEX

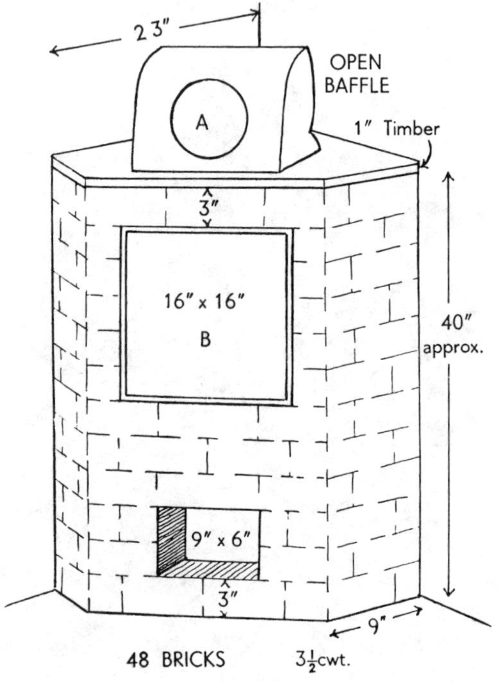


In this double-speaker system, a non-resonant corner cavity has been achieved at low cost by a panel of bricks and cement, completed by a heavy wooden top or lid. The bass speaker is a 15-inch unit with cloth suspension. The cone resonance is down to 18 cycles at which frequency the port emission blows out a lighted match with only 2 watts input to speaker. The cavity of 9 cubic feet gives air-column resonance just above 50 cycles. A ten inch cloth surround unit on open baffle is used for treble, with useful reflection from corner walls. The usual cross-over at 1,000 cycles is adopted. The reproduction of speech and music is far superior to anything possible with smaller or less rigid structures.

The 23″ dimension on the diagram indicates the internal measurement.

The remarks about 5″ unit and felt partition which are made on the previous page would apply with equal force to the above installation.

# KLIPSCH-HORN

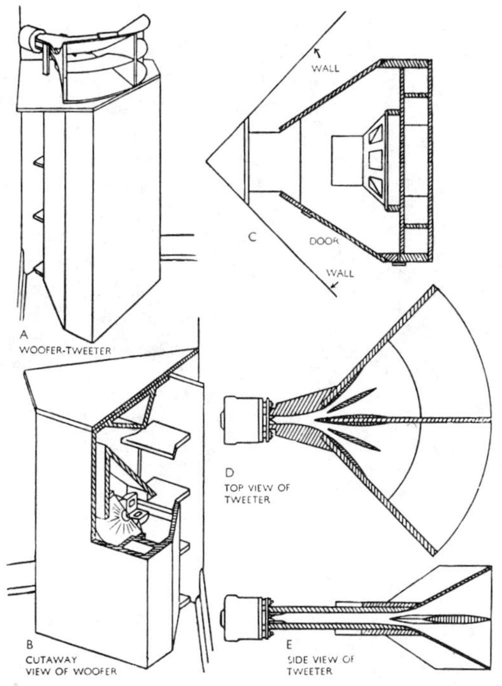


*Reproduced from Journal of the Acoustical Society of America, by courtesy of Vitavox Ltd.*

The Klipsch design is an interesting adaptation of exponential horn loading to dimensions suitable for domestic use. The corner of the room acts as an extension of the low frequency flare, and efficiency down to 30 cycles is claimed with a suitable 15-inch driving unit. A cross over at 400/500 cycles is used. The H.F. horn consists of a multi-cell arrangement for a short distance, followed by single horn expansion in a different plane.

# GOODMAN'S AXIOM 80

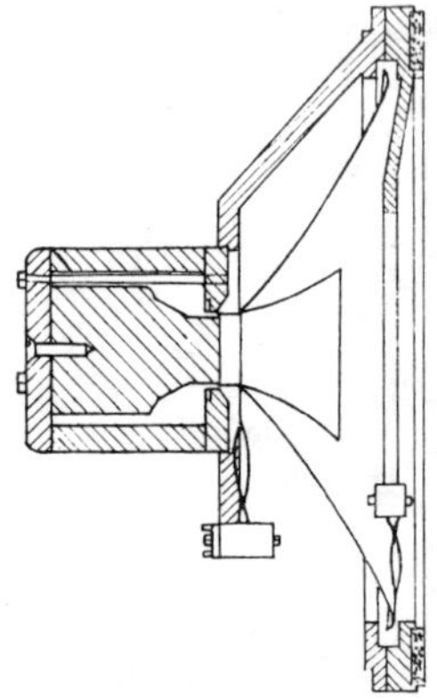

The diagram illustrates an interesting twin-cone free-edge speaker, having the remarkably low resonance of 25 cycles on large baffle. When used in totally enclosed cabinet the resonance rises to 40 c/s with 4½ cu. ft. or 50 c/s with 3½ cu. ft. enclosure. Special gap design gives 17,000 lines flux density, the suspension is on the Duplex Cantilever principle, and response is maintained up to 20 k.c. The free-edge avoids "surround" resonances and greatly reduces cabinet resonance. Chassis diameter 9½″, peak input 10 watts, total flux 62,600 lines, weight 9 lbs.

# TANNOY DUAL CONCENTRIC

Usually known as a coaxial speaker, this design consists of a 15 inch low frequency unit and a horn loaded high frequency unit, with crossover at 1,000 c.p.s. The low frequency cone forms the final section of the high frequency horn, the latter being fitted with a duralumin diaphragm, two inches in diameter. Frequency response 30 to 20,000 c.p.s. Flux density, L.F. 12,000 Gauss, H.F. 18,000 Gauss. Peak input 20 watts. Weight including crossover, 30 lbs. Bass Resonance 35 cycles.

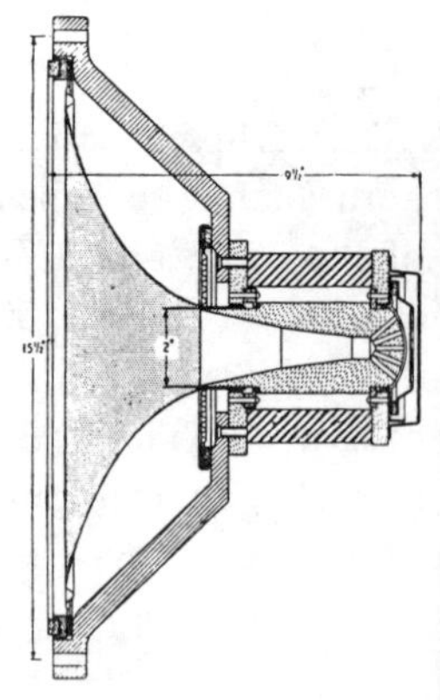

# ELECTROSTATIC SPEAKER

The Electrostatic loudspeaker uses the principle of a condenser. Models were made even twenty or thirty years ago, but were then expected to cover a wide frequency range and severe distortion was produced by the single plate system.

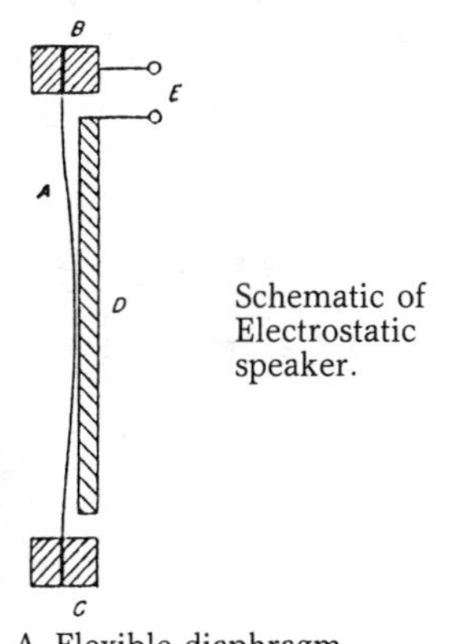


Schematic of Electrostatic speaker.

A Flexible diaphragm.
B and C Clamped supports for A.
D Peforated rigid backplate.
E Input for AC signal and D.C. polarising voltage.

Recent German designs, such as the Körting and Isophon, use the system only for the HF range of 7000-20,000 c/s, thus avoiding the frequency doubling which sets in at lower frequencies. As the impedance of the speaker goes down as the frequency rises, the response is easily maintained to the highest audio limit. A sample tested by the writer showed an impedance of 15,000 ohms at 5 kc/s, falling to about 2,000 ohms at 15 kc/s.

The diagrams show the principle of working. The diaphragm A is maintained by the clamps at B and C; D represents the fixed electrode which is quite rigid; and E shows the points to which the signal and the DC polarisation voltage are applied. The diaphragm A is flexible, but a fine isolating film of elastic substance such as Styroflex prevents contact with D.

## RECENT DEVELOPMENTS

Unfortunately the sensitivity of the above type of E.S. speaker is very low and it can only be used as a tweeter with middle and bass loudspeakers of poor efficiency. During the last two or three years, engineers in several countries have been trying to remove some of these long-standing disadvantages, and considerable progress has been made. (The work of Janszen and Pickering in America, and M. Charlin in France, P. J. Walker and D. T. N. Williamson in Great Britain, should be acknowledged here.)

The improvement has been due mainly to the adoption of push-pull arrangements together with constant charge operation. The moving diaphragm is supported mid-way between two fixed plates which are perforated so as to be acoustically transparent.

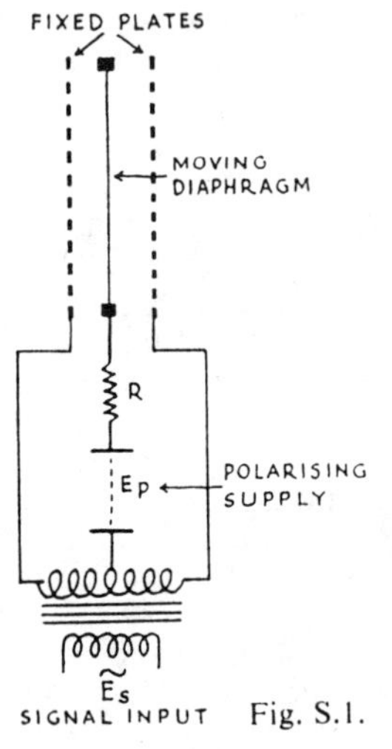

Fig. S.1.

The signal voltage is fed across the fixed plates by a centre tapped transformer and the polarising voltage is applied to the moving diaphragm through a high resistance R. This high resistance acts in conjunction with the capacitance of the system so as to keep the *electrical charge* on the diaphragm constant when it moves to and fro under the action of the applied signal. With former methods of operation, the *polarising voltage* on the diaphragm was kept constant but the *charge* was allowed to vary.

These new arrangements bring some spectacular improvements in performance, among the more important being the reduction of distortion to negligible proportions, even with large excursions of the diaphragm. The risk of breakdown is also very much reduced, since the voltage between the diaphragm and a fixed plate tends to disappear when they come near to touching. Because of the great latitude of design resulting from this new mode of operation, these units can be made to have a sensitivity approaching that of modern moving coil loudspeakers.

The transient response is very good because every part of the diaphragm is subject to the control of the driving force. For the same reason, any tendency for the diaphragm to break up is greatly reduced and its motion becomes mathematically predictable. Thus, an electrostatic loudspeaker may be designed to give good distribution of sound, free from axial beaming effects, without the use of diffusers or acoustic lenses.

Several good designs have already been demonstrated, and the photograph of Fig. S.2. shows a prototype unit by the Acoustical Manufacturing Company Ltd. of Huntingdon, which handles the full range of audio frequencies with two separate loudspeakers fed through a dividing network. The results are very good indeed and give some idea of what one may expect from these units when their development is finalised.

Fig. S.2.
First Electrostatic Speaker covering the full audio range of 40 to 14,000 c/s. Made by Acoustical Manufacturing Co. Ltd., Huntingdon, and demonstrated in London in May 1955. Height 5ft. overall.

Such a wide range E.S. speaker is difficult and costly to produce and is not yet a commercial proposition. One problem is the design of suitable enclosures to obtain proper radiation of the low frequencies. Units to operate at frequencies above about 1 kc/s are however within sight, and will undoubtedly appeal to amateurs who will not object to taking the steps required to provide the D.C. polarising voltage (in spite of the fact that this small burden soon allowed the permanent magnet to knock the mains energised moving coil speaker out of the audio ring.)

# THE ELIPSON

The Conque Elipson is an invention of Mr. Lèon, of Paris. The shell acts as a highly efficient reflector of sound energy produced by a normal moving coil loudspeaker. The reflector is part of an elongated ellipsoid which ensures the concentration and diffusion of the sound for all frequencies above 800 c/s. The classical laws of reflection of light waves are valid so long as the wavelength of the sound is less than the greatest dimension of the reflector. The next diagram shows how a selected area can be covered by the reflected sound, which incidentally reduces echo effects from ceiling or roof in public places.

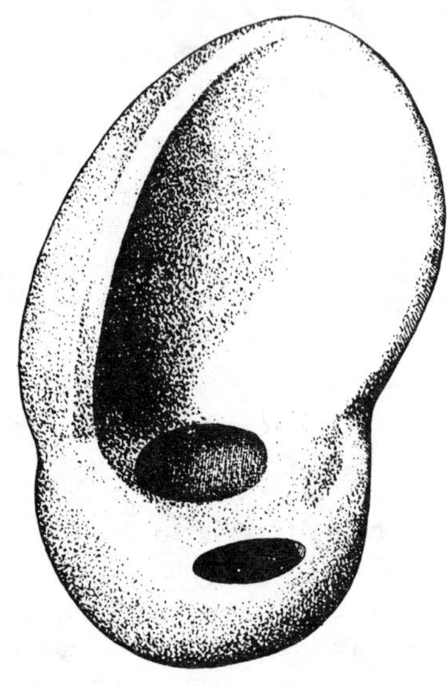

Conque Elipson
British Patent No. 719,969

An installation at the Air Terminal in Paris results in a clarity of speech which is most unusual in such places. An open-air installation at the Palace of Versailles uses a number of Elipson speakers in stereophonic reproduction of speech and music, with remarkable clarity and realism.

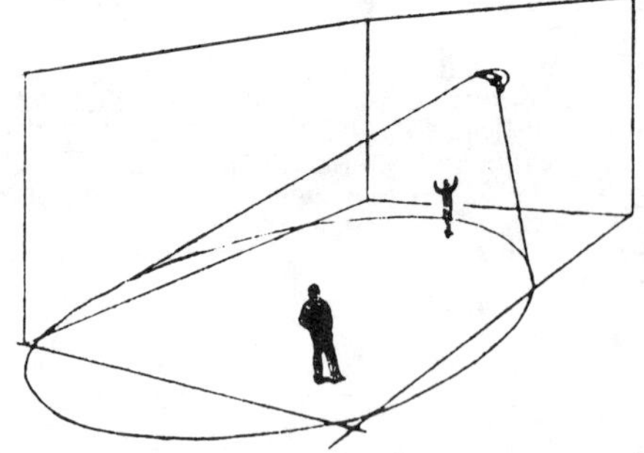

The directivity of the Conque Elipson is speciallv suitable for sound reproduction in locations where acoustic conditions are bad and echo effects are objectionable.

The Elipson could be conveniently used with a crossover network at about 800 c/s. and a separate bass reflex speaker in place of the small Helmholtz Resonator which is shown in the first illustration; or the device could be embodied in a large reflex enclosure to improve sound dispersal in the middle and upper registers.

# INDEX

# INDEX

# BOOKS *from Old Colony Sound Lab*

## BUILDER'S GUIDES, general

| | | |
|---|---|---|
| BKAA-4 | KILLER CAR STEREO ON A BUDGET | $19.95 |
| MH-2 | HOW TO MAKE PRINTED CIRCUIT BOARDS | $8.90 |
| S-25 | ELECTRONIC PROTOTYPE CONSTRUCTION | $17.95 |
| S-27 | DESIGN OF OP AMP CIRCUITS | $12.95 |
| S-32 | HOW TO READ SCHEMATICS | $14.95 |
| T-8 | ENHANCED SOUND—22 Electronics Projects for the Audiophile | $10.95 |
| T-10 | ACOUSTIC TECHNIQUES FOR HOME AND STUDIO | $18.95 |

## SOUND ENGINEERING, REFERENCE WORKS

| | | |
|---|---|---|
| B-1 | LOUDSPEAKER AND HEADPHONE HANDBOOK | $110.00 |
| MH-1 | HANDBOOK FOR ELECTRONICS ENGINEERING TECHNICIANS (2nd Ed.) | $48.95 |
| MH-4 | AUDIO ENGINEERING HANDBOOK | $85.00 |
| NE-1 | NEW EARS: A Guide to Education and the Recording Sciences | $11.95 |
| PH-1 | HANDBOOK OF SIMPLIFIED SOLID-STATE CIRCUIT DESIGN | $39.95 |
| RR-1 | 1990 ARRL HANDBOOK FOR THE RADIO AMATEUR | $23.00 |
| S-19 | SOUND SYSTEM ENGINEERING | $49.95 |
| S-28 | HANDBOOK FOR SOUND ENGINEERS: The New Audio Cyclopedia | $79.95 |
| X-1 | PERCEPTION OF REPRODUCED SOUND | $35.00 |

## GUIDEBOOKS AND DATABOOKS

| | | |
|---|---|---|
| N-5 | VOLTAGE REGULATOR HANDBOOK | $7.00 |
| N-6 | LINEAR DATA BOOK 1 | $16.95 |
| N-7 | LINEAR DATA BOOK 2 | $10.95 |
| N-8 | LINEAR DATA BOOK 3 | $10.95 |
| N-678 | LINEAR DATA BOOKS (3-volume set) | $35.00 |
| P-1 | THE PENGUIN GUIDE TO STEREO RECORDS & CASSETTES | $12.95 |
| P-1A | THE PENGUIN GUIDE TO COMPACT DISCS, CASSETTES AND LPs | $14.95 |
| S-30 | TUBE SUBSTITUTION HANDBOOK | $5.95 |

## BUILDER'S GUIDES, specific (cookbooks)

| | | |
|---|---|---|
| S-9 | REGULATED POWER SUPPLIES | $21.95 |
| S-10 | IC OP AMP COOKBOOK | $21.95 |
| S-13 | AUDIO IC OP AMP APPLICATIONS | $17.95 |
| S-14 | ACTIVE FILTER COOKBOOK | $15.95 |
| S-17 | IC TIMER COOKBOOK | $17.95 |
| S-18 | TTL COOKBOOK | $14.95 |
| S-26 | CMOS COOKBOOK | $18.95 |

## TUTORIAL

| | | |
|---|---|---|
| BKAA-3/1 | AUDIO ANTHOLOGY (Vol. 1) | $16.95 |
| BKAA-3/2 | AUDIO ANTHOLOGY (Vol. 2) | $16.95 |
| BKAA-3/3 | AUDIO ANTHOLOGY (Vol. 3) | $16.95 |
| BKAA-3/S | AUDIO ANTHOLOGY (Vols. 1–3) | $42.00 |
| BKAA-5 | LOUDSPEAKERS: The Why & How of Good Reproduction | $6.95 |
| D-1 | REPRODUCTION OF SOUND | $3.95 |
| D-3 | MUSIC, PHYSICS AND ENGINEERING | $7.95 |
| G-1 | LIVING WITH HI-FI | $7.95 |
| P-8 | INTRODUCING MUSIC | $5.95 |
| S-4 | UNDERSTANDING IC OPERATIONAL AMPLIFIERS | $12.95 |